LANGUAGE AND LITERACY SERIES
Dorothy S. Strickland and Celia Genishi, SERIES EDITORS

* Volumes with an asterisk following the title are a part of the NCRLL set: Approaches to Language and Literacy
Research, edited by JoBeth Allen and Donna Alvermann.

(Continued)

Critical Literacy/ Critical Teaching

TOOLS FOR PREPARING RESPONSIVE TEACHERS

Cheryl Dozier

Peter Johnston

Rebecca Rogers

foreword by JoBeth Allen

TEACHERS
COLLEGE
PRESS

Teachers College
Columbia University
New York and London

Published by Teachers College Press, 1234 Amsterdam Avenue, New York, NY 10027

Library of Congress Cataloging-in-Publication Data

Dozier, Cheryl.
    Critical literacy/critical teaching : tools for preparing responsive teachers / Cheryl Dozier, Peter Johnston, Rebecca Rogers ; foreword by JoBeth Allen.
        p.   cm.—(Language and literacy series)
    Includes bibliographical references and index.
    ISBN-13: 978-0-8077-4646-2 (cloth : alk. paper)
    ISBN-10: 0-8077-4646-0 (cloth : alk. paper)
    ISBN-13: 978-0-8077-4645-5 (paper : alk. paper)
    ISBN-10: 0-8077-4645-2 (paper : alk. paper)
    1. Reading teachers—Training of.   2. Reflective teaching.   3. Critical pedagogy.
I. Johnston, Peter H.   II. Rogers, Rebecca.   III. Title.   IV. Language and literacy series (New York, N.Y.)

    LB2844.1.R4D69   2005
    428.4′071—dc22

                                                                                2005051442

ISBN-13:   ISBN-10:
978-0-8077-4645-5 (paper)   0-8077-4645-2 (paper)
978-0-8077-4646-2 (cloth)   0-8077-4646-0 (cloth)

Printed on acid-free paper

Manufactured in the United States of America

13   12   11   10   09   08   07   06   8   7   6   5   4   3   2   1

Contents

Foreword

Marcus*, a child who became a reader through his participation in the University at Albany Literacy Lab, could barely contain his enthusiasm. "Grandma, you got time? Papa, you got time? I want to read to you." That's the way I felt after I read this book—I keep grabbing colleagues in schools and my department and saying, "Have you got time? I want to tell you about this great book I just read."

Cheryl Dozier, Peter Johnston, and Rebecca Rogers's goal in writing *Critical Literacy/Critical Teaching* was to describe and document an approach for educating literacy teachers so that they become critically literate and also learn to accelerate struggling learners into critical literacy. They accomplish this goal in a creatively crafted, meticulously researched, soundly theorized account of how they engage teachers in the Literacy Lab, and how teachers in turn engage children and their families. Through thorough syntheses of several fields of theory and research, the authors explain concepts (e.g., critical literacy), create an overall framework that shows concepts in relation to each other, and elaborate and illustrate those concepts with comprehensive program description and chapters written by teacher coauthors.

The authors provide a detailed explanation of each aspect of the tutoring sessions their graduate students lead in the Literacy Lab. Teachers use both Reading and Writing Instructional Log/Planning Sheets to think through the texts they will use, how they will introduce and prompt discussion of new books, plans for word study and spelling development—many of the aspects of effective teaching-learning interactions we have learned from Reading Recovery and other one-to-one instructional programs.

The Albany program is both unique and powerful in its focus each

---

**Author's note:* all student and teacher names, as well as Douglass Elementary, are pseudonyms.

session on Critical Literacy. This attention may be new for many teachers and teacher educators in a "remedial" setting. Strong forces in educational policy and publishing doggedly portray literacy as apolitical, ahistorical, decontextualized skills acquisition, especially for children least successful in demonstrating school literacies. However, Cheryl, Peter, and Rebecca enact their explicit goal for teachers and students to "engage in literacy critically and purposefully [and to] approach learning with an expanding sense of social justice and social agency." Through reading, class discussions, and the section on the planning form labeled "Critical Literacy," teachers reconceptualize and help students think critically about texts and contexts, authority and agency, prejudice and power in the lives of book characters, as well as their own.

The authors explain complex and sophisticated conceptual and pedagogical tools for accelerating learning. For example, to develop Tool #2, Home Communication: Learning from Families, teachers in the Literacy Lab engage in multiple pathways for establishing ongoing communication with families, including taking photographs that document students' literate lives and integrating them into the curriculum, collecting family stories, dialoguing in family journals, making home visits, attending community events, and inviting family members to observe and discuss their child during a tutoring session—an invitation that parents realize relates directly to their child's academic development, unlike many "parent involvement" programs.

In another unique feature of the book, teachers write about their experiences after they graduate and go beyond their Literacy Lab experiences. For example, Jennifer Grand, embracing the concept of forming a respectful partnership with family members, invited parents of her middle school students into The Parent and Teacher Book Group. She is not there to teach "parenting skills" or ask parents to get their children to comply with school rules. Parents and teachers together select, read, and discuss adolescent literature so they can talk about books with their children over the dinner table, brainstorm ways of engaging both avid and reluctant readers, evaluate the appropriateness of controversial books for their own children, and enjoy reading and discussing literature as equals.

Marilyn Cochran Smith as editor of the *Journal of Teacher Education* identified that one of the greatest needs in teacher education research is to learn what teachers do after they graduate—what difference does an innovative program or an extended field experience make? This book fulfills that challenge better than any research on teacher education I know.

As you turn the page now to read *Critical Literacy/Critical Teaching*, we close in the spirit of LaShandra, who learned with tutor Vanessa la Raé (chapter 14) that becoming a reader meant in part finding books she really wanted to read. As LaShandra said to Vanessa I say to you with equal fervor: "You brought a good book to read today. Hallelujah! Praise the Lord!"

JoBeth Allen

Acknowledgments

This book has served as a tool that has helped us expand our thinking about literacy teaching and learning, and teacher education, toward a more just society. At the same time, it serves as a monument to the many, many people who have been instrumental in advancing our theory and practice.

A special thanks goes to Eva Joseph for sharing our enthusiasm in moving the lab from the university to Douglass Elementary School. We met on a spring day, with an idea in hand, and as we worked to implement the program, she provided support, encouragement, and appropriate contacts for us to do our teaching and research in the elementary school. Our work would not have got off the ground without the support of Bob White, the building principal, Michele Bridgewater, who started the process, Willard Williams, the after school program coordinator, Mary Ellen Kavenaugh, Jerselle Nasib, and Megan Fabio, reading teachers in the building, and all of the teachers at Douglass Elementary who worked with us to implement the program.

We could not do this work without our stellar graduate students who co-teach with us and help us become better teachers and researchers of our own practice. Our deepest appreciation goes to the children who participated in the tutorials, their families, and the teachers who wrote chapters for the book. It is because of them that we continue to find inspiration in the work we do. And, of course, we are indebted to the countless other people who we have not named but who work, tirelessly, in the school for the children.

Our respective institutions have each provided us with support in the form of colleagues who cared about this work and provided encouragement, and occasional funding. Although all the faculty in the Reading Department at the University at Albany play a role, those most closely associated with supporting and extending the literacy lab are Brian Burr, Barbara Gioia, Ginny Goatley, Sherry Guice, Cindy Lanford, Erin McClosky, Ilene Rutten, Lisa Strolin-Smith, Sean Walmsley and Trudy Walp. These colleagues not only make the course possible, their ideas, enthusiasms, critiques, and uniqueness fuel its evolution. At Washington University in St. Louis Peg Finders, Phyllis Balcerzak, and Bill Tate remind us that teaching teachers really can be a revolutionary act. Dr. Cynthia Warren, principal of the elementary school in St. Louis, has supported and encouraged Becky to set up a similar literacy lab, where she continues the line of work set forth in this book. A special thank you goes to Dean Sue Phillips at the University at Albany, who takes our work seriously and advocates for us.

Our work has also found a supportive community in the Clinic/ Literacy Lab study group at the National Reading Conference. Penny Freppon, Barbara Laster, and Terry Deeney have been particularly encouraging.

JoBeth Allen and an anonymous reviewer provided helpful feedback along the way. We also greatly appreciate JoBeth's generous foreword for this work. And, we owe a special thanks to our editors Carol Collins, Wendy Schwartz, and Aureliano Vázquez. The book is more readable because of the thoughtful editorial comments we received.

Finally, this book, at its core, rests on the love and support of each of our families. They are a constant reminder of the beauty of humanity that grounds the work we do.

Part I

THE FOUNDATIONS OF OUR TEACHING AND INQUIRY

In this first section of the book we introduce the theoretical foundations of our work. In Chapter 1, we offer the logic and motivation of our inquiry into our teaching. We describe the parallels we see among teaching, literacy, and researching our practice. We also describe the parallels we see across layers of our Literacy Lab teaching-learning experience—students, teachers, and teacher educators.

Chapter 2 explores the logic of teaching for the twin goals of acceleration and critical literacy. It clarifies the demands of this teaching and the obstacles that must be overcome.

Chapter 3 explores the significance of case studies and a critical awareness of language. The central thread throughout this first section of the book is critical and collaborative inquiry into language patterns, histories, and practices and their contexts and consequences.

1

Researching and Teaching with Literacy Teachers

It is our responsibility and privilege to teach literacy teachers. It is a responsibility we find rewarding, challenging, and constantly educative. We offer this book both in celebration of teaching, and as an invitation to participate in the rich space of inquiry and practice that responsive teaching offers. This book is a study of the multilayered complexity and evolution of a capstone practicum class in a master's degree program designed to prepare literacy specialists. Its evolution has been fueled over the years by the collaborative efforts of a range of thoughtful teacher educators and has escalated in the past 5 years as our research efforts have focused more systematically on the process and consequences of our practice.

CALLS FOR THIS RESEARCH

This book was prompted, in part, by a number of recent calls for action. In 1996 the National Commission on Teaching and America's Future observed that universities often do not practice what they preach in terms of teaching. The criticism did not sit well with us. Aside from the fact that we try not to preach too much at all, we work hard to align our expectations for our own and our students' practice. It is true that as a profession we have not publicly articulated the nature of this alignment as much or as clearly as we might. We hope to remedy this in the chapters that follow.

Our particular practice involves teaching teachers of literacy, an area that needs to be well-articulated. Indeed, Anders, Hoffman, and Duffy (2000) open their chapter in the *Handbook of Reading Research* (Vol. III) with the question, "How should teachers be taught to teach reading?" (p. 719). They conclude from their review that neither re-

3

search on in-service nor preservice teaching "explains how teachers of reading are created, how they teach, nor how they change" (p. 732). They offer a research agenda in the form of the following "unresolved problems": "How do we teach problem solving? What assignments and activities make sense? What beliefs are productive, and how can we get to them? And how can we prepare teachers for the students they will face?" (p. 734). They conclude that the necessary research will involve "commit[ting] our energies to studying our programs, our courses, our teaching, and our expectations and requirements. In short, it means consenting to be the subject of study ourselves" (p. 734). This book is a response to their call.

Anders and her colleagues (2000) are not the only ones calling for research on literacy teacher development. Hoffman and Pearson (2000), reviewing the status of teacher education in literacy, present an agenda for the "reading teacher education community" that includes taking a leadership role in generating a research agenda, building a database on reading teacher education, developing assessment systems for productive evaluation of teacher education, creating spaces for dialogue and deliberation on the issues, and making sure that one of the issues is diversity.

Coincident with these calls for increased research on the education of literacy teachers, there are concerns about the nature of the research that has been done. Anders and her colleagues (2000), for example, note that the available research has focused primarily on the content of courses rather than on the ways the courses are taught, as if teaching knowledge were merely factual knowledge. It is not.

RESEARCH/TEACHING AGENDA

We align ourselves with the traditions of teacher research (Cochran-Smith & Lytle, 1993; Fishman & McCarthy, 2000; Knoblauch & Brannon, 1988; Lytle, 2000) and action research (Kemmis & Wilkinson, 1998; Noffke, 1995; Zeichner & Gore, 1995). Indeed, we view our teaching of this class as an ongoing action research project, primary components of which include inquiring into one's own activity and situation, collaboration, and an emancipatory/democratic intent (Schuyler & Sitterly, 1995).

Collectively, we have experience with a range of approaches to research that we draw on and from as we research our practice in the lab. We have experience with, among other forms of research, case studies (Johnston, 1985; Johnston & Backer, 2002; Johnston, Bennett,

& Cronin, 2002; Johnston & Quinlan, 2002), ethnographies (Rogers, 2002, 2003), discourse analysis (Johnston, 2004), critical discourse analysis (Rogers, 2002, 2004), and teacher research (Dozier, 2001). This draws our attention at once to the detail of the case, the significance of language and context, and the consequential and value-laden role of the researcher and the act of doing research. The very act of investigating our own practice aligns us with work on teacher research. We very much value both the empirical and the intuitive knowledge we and our teachers bring to the teaching-researching process.

In drawing on different research traditions and their associated methods, we emphasize how each tradition offers a different lens for problem-solving and theory-building. For example, the thick description of ethnographic work combined with the attention to language and discourse analysis and the reflexivity associated with teacher preparation research add up to more than their sum.

ALIGNING OUR RESEARCH AND TEACHING

We also take the position that action research is exactly what teaching and teacher education involve. This common frame is important to us as we try to evolve a coherent praxis. Viewing the overall enterprise this way provides coherence, but simultaneously reveals both the complexity and the political nature of the undertaking. Kemmis and Wilkinson's (1998) view also reinforces knowing more than merely accumulating knowledge. In other words, although we are interested in the possibility of generating knowledge that can be useful to others, the central aspect of our research is individual and locally contextualized development.

Our approach to research is consistent with our instructional practice in other ways, too. First, we emphasize the use of inquiry-based case study methods in both research and teaching. Second, we emphasize language awareness at all levels. Third, we take an action orientation to our work, at each level working to build a sense of agency. Fourth, at each level we are concerned with context and consequences.

INSIDER-OUTSIDER RESEARCH

Although the insiderness of teacher research is very important, we believe collaborative teacher research is productive for a number of reasons. First, human beings have a tendency to avoid disconfirmatory analysis (Wood & Wood, 1996). We tend to see what we expect (and want) to see and filter out conflicting information. Second, a central stimulus for learning is the discomfort provided by disjuncture—often the discrepancy between different perspectives. Consequently, insider-outsider research holds some advantage. Fishman and McCarthy (2000), in their efforts to do insider-outsider research, make the argument that their collaborative efforts have forced them to integrate their respective narrative and analytic stances on classroom research and that their work is the better for it. We argue the same and that, as they also show, productive collaboration requires particular social relationships—ones that enable and expect addressing disconfirming evidence and contrasting perspectives. From our perspective, developing teacher research requires building a sense of how to develop such relationships, and an attitude of inquiry and exploration more than truth-testing. Because of another human failing, the tendency to rely on memory (Wood & Wood, 1996), we also build habits of data collection and analysis.

We are actively involved in working with both teachers and students, and our ongoing hypotheses and data influence our continued practice and their lives. Realization of the consequential and value-laden aspect of both teaching and researching requires us to view our work ideologically. This in turn insists that we view our work as action research in the tradition of Kemmis and Wilkinson (1998), Smyth (1987), and others (Noffke, 1995; Zeichner & Gore, 1995) whose work centers on teachers and schools. We also must adopt this position with our teachers.

In this we differ from Fishman and McCarthy (2000), who argue that requiring that teacher research adopt an ideologically focused position might discourage research on less charged issues like classroom management, or how to encourage high school students to read. Our position is that research is always ideological, and recognizing that fact requires teachers and researchers to think through the implications of their efforts. As with other action researchers, we align ourselves with efforts to advance democratic and social justice agendas. We are guided by Collins's (1998) notions of "visionary pragmatism" that integrate the possibility of acting in the world as it is (inequitable), without losing sight of the world as it might be (equitable and just). Happily, this also aligns well with our views on literacy teaching and learning.

We encourage this theorizing in our teachers and expand it by involving recent graduates in the teaching/research side of the program. Our goal for this book is to encourage it further by providing productive frameworks and teaching tools.

ORGANIZATION OF THE BOOK

Part I of this book provides the framework and context for our work. In this chapter we have described the logic of our research agenda. We hope we have also convinced you of the pressing need for such work. Chapter 2 explores the logic of our instruction and its foundations in critical literacy and Marie Clay's (1993) teaching for acceleration. In chapter 3 we attend to the centrality of language choices in our work and detail the goals of the program for teachers, students, and ourselves, and the relationships among those goals.

Part II focuses directly on our teaching practice to explore the very practical teaching tools and processes we use to accomplish our goals. Each of the teaching tools is designed to provide both conceptual and social leverage—to be vehicles for socializing productive interactions. In teaching children we are guided by Vygotsky's (1978) view that "children grow into the intellectual lives of those around them" (p. 88). With teachers we are guided by the corollary—Teachers grow into the intellectual lives of those around them.

Part II also contains illustrative case examples from teachers who have graduated from the Literacy Lab, thus providing concrete examples of teaching and learning that are the center of our practice. These cases represent a range of perspectives from teachers just finishing the program to those who have returned as co-instructors. Each chapter written by a teacher presents a different focus, ranging from the integration of knowledge into the curriculum, to the importance of language choices, to the transfer of knowledge from the lab to subsequent teaching in schools.

Part III of the book considers teacher change and the evolution of the program. In the final chapter, we pull together the threads of the book, describe our current problem-solving, and present a prospective look at the trajectory of our work. We will argue that there are productive parallels between the research, teaching, learning, and literacy traditions on which we have drawn, and describe our efforts to resolve tensions in our teaching among sometimes competing theoretical frameworks.

AUDIENCE FOR THIS BOOK

We wrote this book primarily for others like ourselves who are involved with teacher education, and with whom we wished to share our thinking and our practice. For these readers we have laid out a curriculum framework for, and a way of thinking about, preparing literacy teachers. We also provide a way of theorizing about and extending *their* teaching. Many of the teaching tools described in the book and much of the logic will be equally valuable for professional staff developers, literacy coaches, and curriculum directors, and not only in the field of literacy. We believe that the tools and logic provide useful practices and metaphors for educating teachers in other domains such as science or social studies. Teacher study groups, too, will find the examples and practices in many of the chapters, not just the teacher chapters, directly applicable to their learning and teaching. Indeed, 9 of the 16 tools apply directly to responsive classroom practice. Similarly, administrators and others charged with observing and evaluating teachers might well find the tools valuable for developing responsive teaching.

2

Critical Literacy, Accelerating Literacy

In the United States, the population of teachers is predominantly white, female, and middle-class, while the population of students in our schools is increasingly diverse (Ladson-Billings, 1994). Our program is no exception. This difference is growing (Darling-Hammond & McLaughlin, 1999) and is magnified for reading teachers since, for a number of reasons, minority students and boys are more commonly identified as encountering, or being at risk of encountering, difficulties acquiring literacy (Peyton-Young, 2001; Smith & Wilhelm, 2001). Consequently, there have been many calls for "culturally conscious" (Wolf, Ballentine, & Hill, 2000), "culturally responsive," or multicultural teaching (Banks, 2003; Banks & Banks, 1995; Gay, 1995; Ladson-Billings & Tate, 1995), all of which involve examination of assumptions and beliefs about culture and learning and the moral and ethical aspects of teaching (Beyer, 1996; Fecho & Allen, 2002; Kerr, 1996; Tappan, 1998). Yet studies have suggested that mere coursework in multicultural education has limited power to change preservice teachers' cultural understandings (Goodwin, 1997), and many student teachers report feelings of helplessness in confronting issues of cultural difference because of their limited exposure to anything other than white, middle-class cultures. The problem, as Cole and Knowles (2000) put it, is that "we teach, research, and otherwise practice what we know and feel. In short, we teach . . . who we are" (p. 188).

THE HURDLES OF HISTORIES

Teaching from a narrow cultural perspective severely limits teaching, particularly, but not only, in classrooms in which children do not share the teacher's culture. But addressing cultural understandings is complicated by the fact that mainstream culture is largely invisible to those who are natives of it. Many don't feel comfortable exploring

9

their own or anyone else's culture because it raises issues of identity and privilege, making them vulnerable as teachers and learners (Goodwin, 1997).

Our teaching project, then, involves uncomfortably changing who people are: their identities. Indeed, we assume that we are educating the whole person and that social and affective dimensions are fundamentally involved (Freppon, 2001). All participants in our community of practice (Lave, 1996) are in the process of crafting identities and co-constructing knowledge and experience. Consequently, our instruction is always intended to be transformative. We are asking teachers to reenter a context, the school, with which they have extensive familiarity and to see it with different eyes. Most of the teachers have been quite successful in the school context; therefore, unless their autobiographical histories and epistemologies are disrupted, they will perpetuate the status quo.

The context in which these teachers have been successful represents a particular type of literacy, what Cook-Gumperz (1986) refers to as "schooled literacy." That is, students learn skills and strategies that are often decontextualized, but also, they learn how to be particular types of people, in a process that Moje (1997) refers to as "studenting." For example, a common request from our teachers early in the class is: "Just tell me what to do." As hooks (1994) put it, "most of us were taught in classrooms where styles of teaching reflected the notion of a single norm of thought and experience, which we were encouraged to believe was universal" (p. 35). Some of the resulting obstacles include:

- A narrow technical, hierarchical, and monological view of literacy, including a systemic concern for conventions over meaning and personal involvement.
- Separation of in-school and out-of-school literacies.
- A view of teaching as telling.
- Unproductive representations of students couched in a language of deficit, standards, and normative frameworks that force attention to difficulties rather than assets.
- A goal of avoiding the display of incompetence.

As we go through our notes each semester, one of our primary objectives is to consider the teachers' language choices and how teachers represent the children they work with. A powerful way of reflecting this initial set of beliefs and values is through a "data poem." A data poem is a form of representation that brings together multiple voices around a central theme. It allows readers to invoke their own interpretations from the actual words of the participants (Hymes, 1991; Peck, 2000). The following data poem draws examples from conversations in the beginning classes.

> Difference
> These are not like my kids.
> How will I know what to talk to him about?
> He should know all his letters. He's in second grade.
> Don't ask me what I think, tell me. You're supposed to know
> more about this than me.
> My job as a teacher is to focus on my students,
> not their families.
> I don't see color.
> I almost didn't come because I had to come here [to
> this urban school].
> My student is so lazy. He resisted everything.
> What if the parents ask me why I am talking about slavery
> with their child?
> What do you mean, "follow the lead" of the child?
> I look at his paper and all I see are the mistakes. I
> forget to see what he is doing right.

CHANGING HISTORIES

Our responsibility is to educate teachers who are capable of accelerating the learning of students who experience the greatest difficulty acquiring literacy. We take this very seriously in terms of its implications for what they teach, how they teach, whom they teach, and the longer-term trajectories of their learning after they have left us. However, our teachers bring with them deeply socialized discursive histories, highly practiced discursive routines, and tightly woven beliefs, values, and discursive practices that do not always frame students productively. Unlearning these language practices and their affective and relational components is at least as difficult as establishing new learning.

Although we wish to influence teachers' instructional goals and practices, the language of representation and interaction is a particular concern for us. We need our teachers to change the ways they use language to represent and to interact with children and each other. Since most people use language without being aware of their choices, we have to bring language choices to awareness in order to change them. Language practices also have to be brought to awareness in a way that *enables* them to be changed. We are mindful that confronting language practices in a way that produces defensiveness will not be productive.

It is not enough, then, for us to have instructional goals that address teaching skills. We must consciously address the relationships, dispositions, and values involved. We would be seriously remiss, for example, to address the skills of teaching literacy without the values of social justice. This is particularly true when most of our teachers are white and middle-class and the students they teach are not, and when much of what students will read reflects a gendered, classed, racist society.

AGENCY

We want our teachers to understand that through their teaching practice they can have an impact on others: students, teachers, schools, and society more generally. This is often referred to as agency: the idea that by acting thoughtfully, one might actually effect change (Johnston, 2004). We believe that this thread connects all layers of our work with teachers, students, and our own teaching and research. Indeed, the concept of agency is central to the action research in which this book is grounded (Kemmis & Wilkinson, 1998). Agency can be viewed as essentially a personal narrative in which the self is a protagonist who confronts and solves problems, with associated motives and affect.

Teachers need a sense of agency in their teaching, their learning, and their literacy. For example, teachers must develop a sense of competence and authority—a sense that they know how to help children to become literate, and how to position themselves productively in discussions about literacy and children's literate development. They cannot view some children as constitutionally beyond the reach of their strategic practice.

Consequently, we as their instructors must ask ourselves whether we make it easy for them to learn more about their teaching, learning, and literacy. Since they will have to constantly formulate and solve problems in their teaching practice when they have left the program, we must have them do this in a productive learning space within the program. This is not only so that they will progressively solve more complex problems, but also so that they understand how to produce the social arrangements that make this continued development possible. Consequently, we need to have our teachers either acting or inquiring into what they might do, using each other as collaborators in the inquiry process, and our language has to foster the development of agency and inquiry.

Teachers must similarly bring this agency to children. For example, when a child figures out an unknown word, it opens the possibility of accepting responsibility for this strategic action, a possibility that is increased when the teacher reviews the event as an agentive narrative (Johnston, 2004)—"You used the picture and checked the letters and *you* figured it out." Accepting this active role in learning and problem-solving is particularly important, and it comes, Clay (1993b) argues, when the child, "takes over the learning process and works independently, discovering new things for himself inside and outside the lessons. He comes to push the boundaries of his own knowledge, and not only during his lessons" (p. 9). Once students do this, they can take an active role in their own development (Schaffer, 1996). So, too, with teachers.

This sense of agency comes out of the experience of successfully participating in these activities and building a productive narrative explaining that success. Consequently, Clay (2001, p. 25) notes that teachers should ask themselves, among other questions, "Do I make it easy for my students to learn more for themselves about how words work?"—and, we would add, about how language works, about how learning happens, and about how teachers can make a difference.

ACCELERATION

Our primary goal at the Literacy Lab is to produce teachers who can accelerate the literacy acquisition of their students, particularly those *why?* who struggle most with literacy acquisition. We have drawn considerably from the work on Reading Recovery™, an early literacy intervention program for the lowest-achieving first-graders (Clay, 1993b; Lyons, Pinnell, & DeFord, 1993). Though our program is not Reading Recovery, research on Reading Recovery has helped us understand the careful structuring of teaching interactions needed to accelerate children's literate development. It has also helped us understand how to engage teachers in active theorizing about their teaching and children's learning. However, whereas Reading Recovery is focused entirely on first-grade students, in order to prevent the development of serious difficulties, our teachers must address a wider age range, including older children who have experienced confusion and failure that complicate their learning (Clay, 1991a; Johnston, 1985; Kos, 1991).

TEACHING FOR AGENCY AND ACCELERATION

In order to accelerate a student's literacy learning and to produce agency, instruction must be contingently responsive, that is, it must be responsive to the child's learning needs at the time the child needs it (Clay, 1998; Wells & Chang-Wells, 1992; Wood & Wood, 1996). Accomplishing this complex task requires a number of conditions.

Sensitive Observation

First, a teacher needs to know how literacy and learning systems are organized, and thus what to notice about a child's literate activity: for example, knowing how spoken and written language relate to one another, how those relationships are learned, how print and speech genres relate to social practices and intentions, and how this understanding is acquired. In other words, the teacher must become a "sensitive observer" (Clay, 1993b) or a "kid-watcher" (Goodman, 1978), able to articulate and correlate observations of particular children with what is known about literate practice and how literate systems work.

Planning and Cross-Checking

Second, a teacher must have the propensity toward checking and expanding that knowledge, cross-checking their assumptions against children's (and their own) behavior. Doing this requires imagining the logic of a student's literate activities from the student's point of view.

Knowing how literacy is organized—what the student knows, does, and is interested in—makes it possible to choose books and activities that keep students within their zone of proximal development. It also makes it possible to follow the student's lead, which, Clay (1993b) points out, is essential for acceleration to occur. She notes that acceleration happens as "the child takes over the learning process and works independently" (p. 9). In other words, acceleration requires teachers to *plan* instruction so that the student is in control of his or her learning processes.

At the same time, the teachers need to be *prepared* to accommodate a student's new learning or confusion in the learning process. To do this, teachers flexibly and strategically draw on resources and strategies, knowing when to wait for self-correction and how to prompt for strategic behavior. This problem-solving demands an inquiry stance toward all aspects of teaching and learning, including the social and institutional contexts of each.

Respect

The third requirement arises from the fact that the zone of proximal development is not only a cognitive space, but also a social, relational space (Goldstein, 1999; Litowitz, 1993; Tappan, 1998). We require our teachers to generate respectful, caring relationships with students and their families (Goldstein, 1999; Noddings, 1992; Rio & Alvarez, 2002; Tappan, 1998). Children and parents readily detect a lack of respect, so this can mean changing teachers' beliefs and values, not just their behavior.

The teachers' relationships with their colleagues are no less important. Because we want our teachers to continue learning beyond the confines of our program, we want teachers graduating from our program to routinely generate learning conversations with their colleagues, to know what these feel like, to expect them as normal, and to notice their absence. In other words, we want them to know what it feels like when they are in their own zone of proximal development, to value that feeling, and to know how to create and extend it by constructing productive intellectual spaces, or "intermental development zones" (Mercer, 2000).

They will also need to capitalize on individual opportunities for learning, many of which are signaled by error or surprise. This means coming to value error and surprise as productive spaces for learning and self-correction for its contribution to independence and development.

Valuing Errors, Self-Corrections, and Learner Control

The centrality of agency to our view of learning means that we must value error and self-correction, both for what they make possible for the individual's learning, and for what they indicate about difficulty and control. Wood (1998, p. 199, cited in Clay, 2001) makes clear the relationship between self-correction and agency, pointing out

> the disposition to correct oneself is not an attribute of personality or ability. When children know, albeit intuitively, what looks, sounds or feels right, we have reason to be confident that they will self-correct and self-instruct. Children who do not show signs of self-correction, are, I suggest, offering mute testimony to the fact that they do not know what they are doing or where they are supposed to be going.

We argue that this is also true of teachers. We, and they, must value error and self-correction. In part this is about valuing approximation, and thus intention. But it is also about valuing the surprise of error, and thus independent monitoring. Both of these leave learners in control.

Risk, Difficulty, and Control

Students need to try new things—to stick their necks out without feeling the risk is too great, while feeling that much is to be gained from the adventure. Among other things, this means continuous adjustment of difficulty through task selection, presentation, and mediation, so that there are multiple points of entry for different learners with a range of experience. It means providing supportive and mediating language.

The level of difficulty must be such that the learner is able *and prepared* to be in control of the activity. As Holdaway observes, "There is no better system to control the complexities and intricacies of each person's learning than that person's own system operating with genuine motivation and self-determination within reach of humane and informed help" (Holdaway, 1979, cited in Clay, 2001, p. 306). For this to happen, Clay (2001) points out that the task must be manageable, but also allow for error because "it is both the opportunity for error behaviour and the control of the amount of error behaviour which provide the opportunities for self-corrections" (p. 206).

Making Literacy Active

Children and their teachers must both see what they can do with literacy and what it can do for them. Their sense of agency in literacy is influenced by what they think they are doing and why they are doing it. Agency in knowledge production, for example, requires viewing texts "not as fixed and complete objects but as places for discussion, argument, and challenge as well as for enjoyment, information, and pleasure" (O'Brien, 2001, p. 40). Since this exploration and understanding is a lifelong one, it can start small, but we must develop a conceptual base of agency—a frame for subsequent elaboration.

There must be an expectation that literate activity can meaningfully accomplish something. For example, we want teachers and students to understand that authors write *purposefully,* choosing what to include and what not to include, what words and genres to use, what stance to adopt, and how to represent information, characters and settings in order to accomplish their goals. Making these language choices,

whether writing fiction or nonfiction, authors construct not mere reflections of reality, but selective versions of it from particular points of
view. These choices are influenced by what the author believes and is
trying to do, but also by the social and historical circumstances in
which the writing takes place. Our teachers and students must understand these aspects of writing in order to write powerfully and to teach
powerful writers.

Understanding writing this way opens the possibility of similar
agency in reading. Readers can ask how a text might have been otherwise if different decisions had been made by the author. Some of these
can be addressed through instructional practices such as comparing
different versions of the same event, rewriting texts in various ways
(adding, deleting, or rephrasing), or role-playing. Learning to exercise
agency in reading also requires expanding the reader's social imagination. For example, students can be asked to imagine why the author
made this choice: how someone else might fill in the gaps differently;
what the author imagined people would know or think; how someone
in a different time or place might think differently; or whose perspective is not represented in the text. Just as we require our teachers to
point to evidence to justify their statements about children's reading
and writing development, we expect them to point to evidence to justify their responses to course readings. Children, too, learn to articulate
the basis of their readings, even in the early stages when they are
asked to cross-check their reading against print, syntax, illustrations,
and their experience.

Agentive learning best occurs in the process of actually accomplishing a valued task or participating in a valued activity. That is not
to say that an aspect might not be taken out of the activity and re-
hearsed separately on some occasions, provided that the rehearsal is
seen as part of, and contributing to, the ongoing action. However,
agentive learning requires task participation always to be manageable yet challenging so that learners get plenty of practice in contexts
that maintain engagement and their control of learning and problem-
solving. This means, for example, that the teachers are selecting books
that are both of appropriate difficulty at the word level and relevant
to the child's interests.

CRITICAL LITERACY

As children are apprenticed into literacy, they acquire more than mere
sets of skills (Banks, 2003; Gee, 1997; Holland & Quinn, 1987; Richardson, 2003; Tomasello, 1999). In becoming literate, they are acquir-

ing ways of interacting with print and of who they are in relation to others in the context of print. They are learning how to be literate, what it means to be literate, what counts as literate practices and conversations (e.g., who gets to ask and answer questions), and what one can do with literacy.

In other words, although our teachers must accelerate children's literacy learning, not just any literacy will do. The students we work with are those most likely to be oppressed by normal schooled literacy (Collins & Blot, 2003; Rogers, 2002). Consequently, our teachers must be prepared to accelerate the acquisition of a *critical literacy* (Banks, 2003; Comber, Thompson, & Wells, 2001; Lewis, Ketter, & Fabos, 2001; Lewison, Flint, & Sluys, 2002; Richardson, 2003). As many scholars have pointed out, there is no neutral literacy (Collins, 1998; Dewey, 1985; Gee, 1996; Kelly, 1995; Richardson, 2003; Smitherman, 2000). All literacies serve particular social functions, and students can acquire a literacy that fits them well for developing and participating in a democracy, or for a very different kind of society. In our view, critical literacy is necessary and fits well with teaching for acceleration, particularly because both emphasize agency.

For us, critical literacy involves understanding the ways in which language and literacy are used to accomplish social ends. Becoming critically literate means developing a sense that literacy is for taking social action, an awareness of how people use literacy for their own ends, and a sense of agency with respect to one's own literacy.

TEACHERS AND CRITICAL LITERACY

To teach critical literacy, our teachers must become critically literate themselves, value social justice, and have a sense of the cultural contexts in which they work. Fennimore (2000) calls for just such programs, arguing that "successful teacher preparation programs need to be constructed upon commitment to activism as well as to excellence in pedagogical practice" (p. 105).

Part of critical literacy requires stepping outside one's self and the social and linguistic structures in which one is immersed. To make change, our teachers have to come to view their current language-saturated realities—views of learners, teaching, and parent involvement—as temporary, as one of many changeable possibilities. They must also recognize these worldviews as value-laden and as connected to their language, and to develop, in Giroux's (1983) terms, a "language of possibility" (p. 9). We cannot, of course, critique all assumptions and aspects of practice at once, but we should "continue to see everything as open to critique at some point, and we should always be working at problematizing something" (Tripp, 1998, p. 37).

CRITICAL LITERACY AND SOCIAL ACTION

Critical literacy also requires understanding literacy as a tool for social action and understanding the ways in which that tool works—for example, how language is organized to reproduce race, class, and gender roles, as well as how language and literate practices are orchestrated to construct liberatory texts (Fairclough, 1992; Luke, 2004). To bring these dimensions of language to teachers' awareness, we include in our class *Rethinking Our Classrooms* (Bigelow, Christensen, Karp, Miner, & Peterson, 1994) and other materials from *Rethinking Schools*, and various articles that emphasize critical language awareness (e.g., Alvermann & Xu, 2003; Comber et al., 2001; Denos, 2003; Simpson, 1996). These readings include a stance toward socially responsible literacy. Building a full critical understanding of language use without concern for social values would risk conferring a powerful tool that can be used for or against social justice. Adopting this socially nonneutral stance is not without its tensions. Our teachers include many, such as members of particular religious groups, for whom such conversations are uncomfortable and not seen as part of literacy. Most are uncomfortable unpacking privilege and its maintenance through literacy.

CRITICAL LITERACY AND ACCELERATION

There are some tensions between our stance toward critical literacy teaching and our more immediate efforts to accelerate the children's literacy acquisition. For example, helping teachers and students attend more closely to issues of social justice in teaching can take some time. Some teachers and students reject the idea that social justice has anything to do with either literacy or learning. Similarly, in part, critical literacy involves consciously reexamining comfortable cultural practices and values. This discomfort can draw energy from the primary focus of acceleration. Our practice is to privilege acceleration while establishing a framework for critical literacy.

Although this can require some initial compromise in focus, there is much that is compatible. Noticing conflict (surprise, error, disjuncture, multiple views) is central to both critical literacy and to learning more generally. For example, when children misread a word, Clay (2001) points out the utility of drawing children's attention to the speech-print conflict, but in the context of the productive aspects of the error. A teacher might say, "That does make sense, but what letters would you expect if that were the word?" This sort of prompt helps build agency. As Clay (2001) observes, it "seems to alert children to the problem that, in English, sounds can appear as different spellings, and the same spellings can have different sounds. The implication is 'be ready to be flexible,' and 'if it is not your first choice try an alternative'" (p. 277).

Conflict is certainly good for conceptual change and for the development of flexible processing. Indeed, Clay (2001, p. 208) argues that "it is a function of brains that they note and work on dissonant information until it becomes consonant with what the brain knows from a variety of sources (or until we give up on trying to solve the problem . . .)." We would argue, however, that in the development of mind, and in particular contexts, an individual can learn to attend or *not* to attend to dissonance. Consequently, we encourage teachers and students to notice disjunctures and view them as learning opportunities. We encourage this not only in terms of print and speech, but when we are considering, for example, different perspectives, as when examining characters' motives and writers' intentions to develop critical literacy.

Agency and disjuncture are not the only compatibilities between teaching for acceleration and critical literacy. Both also require developing ways to rewrite or rethink learning histories. Teachers must change their students' learning trajectories so that they learn faster and catch up to their peers. They must also build this new trajectory into their identities as learners, which means changing their relationships to print, and with their peers. As we noted at the beginning of this chapter, we require this of our teachers as well as their students. They must overwrite, or revise, their previous histories of teaching, learning, and cultural participation. Part of this history/trajectory revision for both parties also requires that it extend into the future.

A final overlap between critical literacy and teaching for acceleration lies in their central attention to language: to the ways language works and to the consequences of particular language practices. Indeed, as Clay (2001) points out, children beginning to read and write are already beginning "to examine the language they speak more closely, at all levels" (p. 26).

3

The Centrality of Language

From the beginning, and constantly, we draw teachers' attention to their own use of language in their teaching, and the sources and consequences of their language practices. Aside from being the foundation for literacy, language is the foundation for learning and communication. A substantial part of our work in teaching teachers involves restructuring language use and ways of thinking about language. To begin with, teachers must understand the significance of the representational properties of language. The sense we make of things is constructed in and through language. Language has its impact from the level of perception on up. When we observe teaching, learning, and literate practices, we actively search for what we have been socialized to consider the most important elements in the sensory array and we assign significance to them with the language we have available. Perception itself is intentional (Harre & Gillet, 1994). Just as children find it easy to read what they expect to see given the sense made so far, regardless of the actual print, teachers at all levels impose expected meanings through the language available.

We begin, then, with the premise that language is central to all aspects of our work—literacy, learning, and teaching—and that language both represents and constructs our understandings of the social world. In other words, language is social action, its meaning dependent on the context. First, the ways in which children are represented to teachers, parents, and children themselves has consequences. If a child's behavior draws a representation of "laziness," it will invoke a different response from representations like "uninterested" or "unengaging instruction." A third-grader might be represented as "learning-disabled," or that same third-grader could be said to be "making a spoken word to printed word match and self-correcting from meaning and print on Guided Reading level E books, and representing most consonant sounds in writing." The difference between these representations is substantial, both in terms of the permanence and agency

21

in the representation, and in terms of the instructional utility of the detail.

Second, because the language teachers use in the process of teaching has consequences, we expect them to become very conscious of how language works in the classroom in the moment and over time. We expect this heightened awareness to build agency in their instructional problem-solving. In other words, our teachers must come to understand that talking *is* social action. When we interact with children through language, we are involved in the structuring of their intellect and their developing identities. Social relationships, too, are grounded in language (and vice versa), and if our teachers are to make a difference in institutional structures that affect them, they will need to understand how power operates in language.

As we noted earlier, our teachers bring with them all of the problematic representational language of the society at large. It is common, initially, for them to describe their students using deficit-based language. This affects the ways they and others interact with the students, and consequently the ways in which the students come to understand themselves and interact with others. Changing this language is a primary order of business not only because negative representations constrain instructional interactions and hence growth in literacy and developing identities, but because such representations close rather than open inquiry. This makes them fundamentally undemocratic. And we cannot simply insist on what has been disparagingly dismissed as "politically correct" language (Knoblauch & Brannon, 1993). It is necessary to actually change teachers' way of thinking: as Fennimore (2000) points out, "a truly democratic *habit or disposition of mind* should incline all educators toward a consistent focus on potential and promise" (p. 24).

To transform, language must change at the representational level and the interactional level. We look for changes in the discourse such that children are positioned as respected, knowledgeable people with interests and productive intentions. For example, we look for a shift from "He's always distracted" to "He really is trying hard to do things correctly but doesn't want to take a risk with the words he really wants to use. He has a lot to say about his baby brother. I need to help him see how he can do it."

Since much of our language use in interaction with others is automatic, and thus out of our awareness, we have to bring these language practices back to awareness in order to change them. And they have to be brought back in a way that enables them to be changed. Making teachers aware of their language practices in a way that makes them defensive is unlikely to be productive.

Sometimes the messages and language are not simply in the language, but in the practice. For example, providing an African American child with a steady diet of books that illustrate the qualities of African culture sends the message that they are descendents of greatness along with the invitation to take their place in that greatness.

LITERACY DIFFICULTIES

Educating specialists who can assist the students experiencing the most difficulty in acquiring literacy requires that we take a stance on what that difficulty means. Since 1983 we have used Marie Clay's conceptualization of literacy learning as our framework for students experiencing difficulty. Clay's work focuses on noticing and teaching to the strengths of each learner and toward the development of a self-extending system, that is, teaching dispositions and strategies that will result in children seeking meaning, self-correcting, and actively seeking problems and solutions. We believe that all children can learn to read and write and that an apprenticeship into literacy is the most productive way to think about literacy acquisition (Cambourne, 1995; Holdaway, 1979; Richardson, 1964; Rogoff, 1995; Tharp & Gallimore, 1988). Nonetheless, some children become confused for one reason or another, sometimes, perhaps, because of small differences in their ability to perceive and process language (Clay, 1998; Spear-Swerling & Sternberg, 1996; Vellutino & Scanlon, 1998; Vellutino, Scanlon, & Sipay, 1997). For example, some children initially find it more difficult than others to notice the ways spoken words are made up of sound units (phonemes). They would thus not understand what the teacher meant by "the first sound in a word." As children try to make sense of instruction, these confusions can compound themselves if unaddressed. But the initial language-processing differences are far from terminal. Even children who have quite extreme differences, such as profound deafness, can become literate (Gioia, 2001). As Clay (1987) argued in "Learning to Be Learning Disabled," we believe that more- and less-successful learners are created more through instructional interactions than through constitutional deficiencies (see also Vellutino & Scanlon, 1998). The conceptual confusions and unproductive learning strategies evident in children who experience difficulty acquiring literacy can be prevented or untangled through sensitive, responsive instruction.

Like Clay (1993b), we assume that for such students productive instruction differs in detail, not in principle, from that which is appropriate for normally achieving students. More care must be taken in matching children to books and managing the task and context so that children are kept within a level of difficulty that allows them to regain control of their learning. The instructional conversation in which they are involved must be one that reestablishes their sense of agency— their sense that by acting thoughtfully, they can solve problems. This can only happen when they can in fact experience success. We also assume that developing a "self-extending system" (Clay, 1993b) or an "executive system" (Vellutino & Scanlon, 2002) is as important as developing skills, knowledge, and strategies.

The labels many children bear before coming to our program are not helpful in solving the problems they might face. Quite the reverse: the labels often lead our teachers to begin teaching in ways responsive to the label rather than the student, thus impressing the label's imprint even deeper. Changing this language is a primary order of business not only because negative representations constrain teaching, and hence growth, in literacy and developing identities, but because such representations close rather than open inquiry and hence are fundamentally undemocratic.

VALUING CASE KNOWLEDGE

Many researchers have placed emphasis on case discussion as a central aspect of teacher education (Shulman, 1986; Wade, 2000), and case study methods have strongly influenced both our teaching and our research strategies. Shulman (1986) referred to case knowledge as "knowledge of specific, well-documented, and richly described events" (p. 11). He points out that the advantage of case-based approaches lies in their narrative integration of context and individual. Others have also argued for the value of cases for engagement in problem-solving, opportunities for analysis, and provoking personal reflection (Merseth, 1996). Case discussion provides the opportunity for collaborative inquiry (Cochran-Smith & Lytle, 1993; Johnston, 1989) and for modeling the kind of inquiry genre that can—and does—continue beyond class sessions (Lyons et al., 1993; Richardson, 1990; Silverman, Welty, & Lyon, 1992; Wasserman, 1993).

Developing cases will help our teachers notice, document, and explain with authority how teaching and learning are related for a particular student. This is especially important when students are not living up to schools' increasing literacy expectations and are referred to school psychologists and special educators. Literacy specialists need to become central informants in these conversations. Psychologists and special educators often have a more limited literacy background than that of classroom teachers and literacy specialists, yet their assessments carry more weight in placement and referral decisions.

Our work includes case study analyses of individual participants (both teachers and students), and examination of the discursive interactions between teachers and students and their parents and between instructors and teachers. The case study foundation for our work includes teachers' and students' self-assessments, which in themselves constitute examples of action research and, in that context, examples of reflective practice. In other words, our goal is to help teachers and students build productive, collaborative case knowledge of their own teaching and learning practices and hence productive identities as teachers and learners.

Teachers regularly prepare case summaries regarding their students to present to their peers or to their students' family and teachers. This provides the opportunity for collaborative inquiry (Wade, 2000) in which teachers become "students of their students" (Nieto, 2000, p. 184)—and of their own practice. Thus they are prepared for the problem-solving and theorizing necessary for refining and developing their growing repertoire as public intellectuals. The writing allows teachers to think through their language in slow motion. Multiple case studies build problem-solving flexibility and test the generalizability of theories.

Adapting instruction for a particular child requires knowing what that child knows and how to bring an activity into that child's range (Clay, 1993a; Johnston, 1997; Lyons et al., 1993; Silverman et al., 1992). This means knowing the child and the available instructional resources and having a working theory of how to relate these to one another flexibly. Having this detailed knowledge of one student builds the expectation of constructing such knowledge for all students.

The one-on-one tutoring associated with case studies also makes it very difficult for teachers to duck responsibility. Teachers who have been used to teaching a full class of students find it more threatening to teach just one publicly, because of this increased burden of responsibility. The process of becoming a teacher, while often exhilarating and energizing, is also often frightening and sometimes disturbing, not least because of the increasing realization of the responsibility involved.

The one-to-one tutoring is a space that allows teachers to focus on the detail of their interactions and the consequences of their teaching in a way that is easily obscured in group teaching. It also requires them to notice the details of children's literate development in a way that reminds them of the feelings, concepts, and theorizing of the individual. Coming to know other students in this detail through their colleagues' cases expands their understanding of real individual difference that can be lost in teaching a group. This understanding is the basis of responsive teaching. Despite these advantages, we wrestle with the disadvantage that in practice much of the instruction these teachers will do will involve teaching groups, which requires additional knowledge of how to manage more than one student. We will return to this topic later.

GOALS AND PARALLELS

Throughout the book, we articulate, exemplify, and explain the parallels among the layers of research, teaching, and learning. Although the learning required by teachers and students is not exactly the same, there is a great deal of overlap both in what is to be learned and how it is learned (Lyons et al., 1993). Indeed, as part of our effort to clarify and expand our practice, we often examine the parallels between our goals and practices for students and teachers, and for ourselves. Sometimes the parallels reveal gaps, insights, and reformulations that help us develop our practice. For brevity and conciseness, we present in Table 3.1 a listing of our current goals, offered in the understanding that each time we go through the process of listing them we expect some change. We will describe the means we use to achieve these goals in Part II of the book.

OUR LEARNING

The central thread throughout is critical and collaborative inquiry into language patterns, histories, and practices and their contexts and consequences. We understand that this inquiry must be reflective. At the Literacy Lab, we experience routine reminders that these matters apply just as much to ourselves as to the teachers we teach. We must be constantly alert to our own histories and their curricular impact (Cochran-Smith, 2000). To give one small example, 5 years ago, when we moved the location of our program from the university, where our teachers served a largely middle-class population, to an urban, primarily African American, low-socioeconomic-status elementary school, we continued our practice of encouraging students and teachers to be

TABLE 3.1. Parallel Program Goals for Teachers and Students

Teachers' Goals	Students' Goals
Generate respectful, caring instructional relationships.	Engage in respectful, caring instructional relationships.
Understand and confront learning histories and patterns. Be willing to engage in new and sometimes uncomfortable practices and conversations.	Understand and confront learning histories and patterns. Be willing to engage in new and sometimes uncomfortable practices and conversations.
Know when they are in their zone of proximal development (ZPD) and what to do when they are not, value being there, and be willing to take risks to move forward.	Know when they are in the zone of proximal development (ZPD) and what to do when they are not. Be willing to take risks to move forward.
Generate productive, dialogic learning conversations. Engage in collaborative critical inquiry to problematize productively.	Engage in dialogic learning conversations.
Understand and articulate how literacy and literacy learning are organized.	Understand and articulate how print and literate practices are organized, how learning happens, and how to allocate attention.
Read critically and think critically about teaching and institutional practices. Approach instruction with an expanding sense of social justice and social agency.	Engage in literacy critically and purposefully. Approach learning with an expanding sense of social justice and social agency.
Base instruction on student's learning—follow the student's lead on a productive learning path—and structure activities in the student's zone of proximal development, with students in productive control of their learning.	Engage in making connections. Understand how new learning connects to their previous learning.
Imagine logic from the student's, parents', and colleagues' point of view.	Imagine story, conversation, and argument from another's point of view.
Value error, particularly the partially correct, and surprise as spaces for learning.	Value error and surprise as spaces for learning.
Become strategic in noticing, theorizing, and cross-checking assumptions against children's' and their own literate behaviors. Flexibly draw on a range of routines, prompts, resources, and strategies.	Become a strategic (i.e., self-correcting) and independent learner.
Have a sense of agency about literacy teaching and learning.	Take productive control of literacy and learning.

on a first-name basis. We did not immediately notice this was not the norm in the local culture.

The parallel goals we describe for our teachers and students are also ones we must keep in mind for ourselves. For some years our practicum has provided ongoing research to inform our instructional decision-making (Dozier, 2001; Dozier & Rutten, in press; Gioia, 1998; Johnston, 1983, 1985; Rogers, in press). We have solid grounds for the goals of our program and a well-grounded sense of the parameters we are working with as we attempt to meet those goals. At the same time, we are fully committed to an ongoing program of researching and evolving our teaching practice. At each level we collaboratively examine the practices in which we are mutually engaged, trying to understand and optimize the consequences of our practice.

OUR AGENDA

Our engagement in teaching/researching this way is intended to improve our teaching, our teachers' teaching, and their students' literacy, not just in the narrow sense of improving skill and knowledge, but in the sense of expanding an agenda of literacy and teaching for social justice and democracy. Our intent is to build a critical literacy from the start among children who are the most oppressed by literacy and most likely to be offered a "basic" rather than a critical literacy. We intend to foster instructional circumstances that ask, indeed demand, that teachers, students, and teacher educators engage in practices that disrupt harmful power–knowledge relationships (Fecho, 2000; Lewis et al., 2001). In particular, we are bent on helping participants at each level develop a sense of agency (hence productivity), involvement (not alienation), rationality (productive theorizing), and social justice (Kemmis & Wilkinson, 1998).

We are interested in learning how to maximize our impact on the literate lives of these most fragile students through maximizing our impact on the teaching and learning lives of their current and future teachers. We also seek to explore the tensions and potential trade-offs involved in teaching children and literacy teachers within a democratic and social justice agenda. Accomplishing this requires analyzing the nature and consequences of our teaching practice and the range of issues connected with field experiences in the preparation of literacy teachers over time (case by case and across cases). For example, we want to understand how changes in learning relate to changes in identities for both teachers and the children they work with, and we want to understand the cultural and social implications of teaching critical literacy and critical teaching in a cross-cultural environment. These themes cut across the education of classroom teachers, literacy teachers, and special education teachers, among others.

We should make it clear from the outset as we describe the evolution of our program that there are always bumps and challenges. Since, like our teachers, we cannot change everything at once, we try to maintain an environment in which evolution and problem-solving are possible and expected. The master's degree students (most of whom are already teaching) teach children who are experiencing difficulty becoming literate. We, in turn, are responsible for teaching them. Both sets of teachers are expected to research their own practice (Cochran-Smith & Lytle, 1993; Lytle, 2000) individually and collaboratively. These two layers of teaching and inquiry offer useful parallels and tensions for theory-building and theory-testing.

Part II

TEACHING TOOLS AND PROCESSES

Part II focuses on the details of our teaching practice and explores the tools and processes we use. The chapters alternate between analyses of the nature, logic, and effects of the instructional tools (Chapters 4, 7, 10, and 13) and case studies written by teachers who have graduated from the program (Chapters 5, 6, 8, 9, 11, 12, and 14).

In the tools chapters, we consider changes in perceptions, language practices, and interactions between teachers and students. The chapters are informed by analyses of teachers and students in the program and our role in their development.

The case study chapters provide concrete examples of teaching and learning representing a range of perspectives, from teachers just finishing the program to those who have been teaching awhile and have returned as co-instructors. These are teachers who, from their reflective essays and our subsequent contact with them, seemed likely to address different aspects of their experience (though we left the choice of focus to them). As we expected, their stories illustrate the consequences of their experience with different instructional tools. That is, some teachers found connecting with the family to be key to acceleration. Others found that providing choice accelerated their students' learning.

We view each of the chapters as additional data points in our description of the implications of our instructional program. They also speak to the self-extending systems these teachers have developed—the *inquiry as stance* (Cochran-Smith & Lytle, 2001) perspective—and the generalization of their learning beyond the context of the class. Throughout the chapters, the range of leadership responsibilities they have assumed is evident. Reading them reminds us of our privilege in teaching teachers.

4

Disrupting and Extending Learning Histories

Accomplishing any complex goal requires using appropriate tools. Teaching is no different (Wells & Cheng-Wells, 1992). Our tools are intended to arrange for learners (teacher educators, teachers, and students) to consciously make meaning of their practice—to attend to the data, to theorize about their practice, and to build self-extending learning. Shaping teachers' thinking and acting in this way requires tools that offer intellectual and social leverage. While all of the tools we will describe are both applied and conceptual tools, for some readers some tools will have more direct applicability to their practice, while other tools will provide conceptual leverage for rethinking practice.

Our primary goal as instructors is to develop self-extending and self-correcting teaching and learning in both teachers and students. A self-extending system, a construct elaborated by Clay (1993b), assumes that learners have a range of strategies at their disposal and use these strategies flexibly and competently in new situations. Building a self-extending system entails setting up the conditions where teachers notice, theorize, productively (self-) critique, and build a sustaining learning community. We use a range of tools to accomplish these ends. The tools, which we describe next, have multiple functions, but for convenience we have grouped them into clusters emphasizing disrupting and extending learning histories (Chapter 4); assessing and representing learning (Chapter 7); building learning communities (Chapter 10); and developing reflective teaching (Chapter 13). Table 4.1 provides a summary of the complete set of tools.

In our efforts to teach for acceleration within a critical literacy framework, we ask the teachers to recognize the narrative resources they bring to their teaching identities, and also to take control of their narratives and to play an active role in the reshaping of the cultural

TABLE 4.1. A Summary of the Instructional Tools and Their Functions

Disrupting and Extending Learning Histories

The following set of instructional tools is concerned with disrupting and extending learning histories. These tools facilitate new learning as teachers examine previously held assumptions about literacy and teaching, particularly regarding race, culture, and language.

Tool 1: Teaching contexts: Locating the literacy lab
By deliberately locating the lab in an urban school in a minority neighborhood, teachers are pushed to reconsider their previously held assumptions about urban schools, children, and themselves, and to reconsider ways of interacting with all students.

Tool 2: Home communication: Learning from families
Establishing ongoing/weekly contact with the families of students challenges stereotypes and breaks down fears of the unfamiliar. Through these engagements, teachers recognize and incorporate into the tutorials home and community funds of knowledge.

Tool 3: Matching teachers and students: Disrupting automatic practices
We place teachers with students at different grade levels from those with which they are familiar. This removes barriers of presumed expertise by reducing all to relative novices. It prevents teachers from engaging in unexamined teaching practices.

Tool 4: Critical emphasis: Considering textual and social analysis
We assume that literacy and teaching are both fundamentally political. In order for teachers to be responsible literacy teachers, we require them to own the social and political implications of their work, and to consider how they can teach toward a more just society.

Assessing and Representing Learning

This set of tools is designed to document, analyze, and represent students' literacy learning in detailed and productive ways.

Tool 5: Roaming in the known: Following the learner's lead
"Roaming in the known" helps teachers notice what learners can do rather than what they cannot do, and to follow their student's lead. In the first 3 days of tutoring teachers are required not to teach but to engage in exploring what the child can already do independently and with some support.

Tool 6: Documenting learning: Observing learning
Understanding students' learning through documenting and analyzing various data sources (e.g., running records, student responses to texts, student writing) expands the literate behaviors teachers notice and the ways teachers make sense of those behaviors.

Tool 7: Writing reports and updates: Informing stakeholders
Writing reports to document the student's growth for various stakeholders assists the teachers in recognizing the importance, power, and centrality of their language choices in representing their learner, and in taking productive control of that language.

Building Learning Communities

This set of tools is designed to build learning communities through productive conversations and celebrations. We believe that teachers' learning is as social as that of their students and that their thinking is grounded and internalized in these learning conversations.

Tool 8: Instructional conversations: Developing a community of learners
Engaging in instructional conversations provides the foundation for the teachers to develop a community of learners. The instructional conversations must have specific properties to sustain teacher learning and act as a model for students' learning.

TABLE 4.1. (continued)

Tool 9: Responding to books and articles: Connecting theory and practice
Responding to books and articles, and the subsequent conversations, helps the teachers connect their teaching practices and theories to the theories and practices of others, and to engage in forms of critique.

Tool 10: Celebrating learning: Connecting teachers, students, and families
Celebrating learning through a final performance at the end of the semester involves all participants—students, families, and teachers—and is an extension of daily celebrations during class conversations.

Tool 11: Reflective essay: Synthesizing learning
Writing and sharing a reflective essay during the final class session, teachers examine their internalized learnings from the course and consider the range of ways of engaging in learning.

Developing Reflective Teaching

The last set of tools is intended to provide teachers with the tools and dispositions necessary to continuously improve their teaching in the course and beyond.

Tool 12: Documenting teaching: Learning to notice and name
Documenting teaching helps teachers plan, prepare, and articulate their pedagogical intentions. It also shifts assessment from the individual child to the child in an instructional context.

Tool 13: Reflective journals: Writing to understand teaching
Reflecting on each tutoring session with focused questions assists the teachers to observe, study, and critique their own practices within a productive learning framework.

Tool 14: Observation conferences: Extending practice
Conferring with instructors and colleagues extends the range of pedagogical possibilities for each teacher. These conferences provide a framework for instructional planning as teachers develop, critique, and analyze their teaching.

Tool 15: Videotaped lessons: Conferring with colleagues
Through viewing and analyzing videotaped lessons with colleagues, teachers learn to represent students and other teachers constructively and provide feedback to extend teaching. They also learn to view colleagues as learning resources and to contemplate multiple plausible possibilities.

Tool 16: Analyzing transcripts: Rethinking the language of interactions
By analyzing the transcripts of audiotaped and videotaped lessons, teachers examine their language choices and interaction patterns and consciously consider alternative interactions and their consequences.

---

narratives. Because changes in activity systems come about through contradictions or disjunctures, the tools we have chosen are organized to produce such pivot points. We think of these tools as conceptual and practical points of leverage for orchestrating the parallel lines of learning among the teachers, the students, and the teacher educators in the Literacy Lab.

TOOL 1. TEACHING CONTEXTS: LOCATING THE LITERACY LAB

Our teachers are virtually all white and middle class, and many believe they are culturally neutral and linguistically correct. If they are to successfully teach minority children, they must come to understand language, themselves, and culturally different students and families anew. Reading about cultural and linguistic differences in books and articles will not accomplish the necessary change. We need a more powerful tool to provide the necessary intellectual, social, and cultural leverage. Moving the practicum into a minority school and community can give us this leverage at the same time as serving the interests of the community. As principal Robert White observes:

> As principal of an inner-city school everyone wants to help you. My job is to select outside programs for the school that coordinate with the intentions of the school and are consistent with the needs of the school, otherwise we'd be going in a thousand different directions.

When we first moved the Literacy Lab into an urban elementary school we had teachers (and their parents and spouses) balk at taking the class. There was genuine fear of the unknown. The discomfort is still there for many of our teachers at the beginning of the semester, though the grapevine has reduced it substantially. Occasionally, shootings near the school, or other crime-related stories on the evening news and in the newspapers, spark new concerns. Our teachers are quite open in their class discussions regarding their discomfort and attitudes regarding working in this poor minority neighborhood, but some are uncomfortable documenting their concerns in writing. As one put it, "I wasn't willing to write about it in my reflective essay, but I was very nervous about coming here."

Disturbing as it is for us, most of our teachers had not worked with minority children at all—and hadn't planned to. Neither had they had contact with minority families. These new experiences stimulated a great deal of discussion and new, and often uncomfortable, learning for everyone. For example, in the first semester we were at the school, second-grader Tanequa commented to her teacher, "You're the first white teacher I've ever had." Disjunctures between expectations and experience force a reorganization of thinking. For example, about a third of the way through our first school semester, a fifth-grade student stabbed another student on the way home from school. The media were merciless in their treatment of the incident, which did not happen on the school grounds. The sheer volume of negative coverage associated with the school was combined with misquoting the principal. However, our teachers were already invested in their students and were disappointed and angry at the way the school had been portrayed. Because of their own initial concerns about coming to the school, they immediately anticipated how this would affect subsequent teachers in the program. They offered to share with future participants their experience regarding their safety and comfort in the school, and the safety procedures they used leaving after dark (the same as on the university campus). They e-mailed the department chair accordingly.

In the context of this school, issues of whiteness, racism, and privilege that previously had been abstractions became concrete. Teachers were obliged to ask themselves "Am I racist," and to confront previously unrecognized privilege. Readings from Delpit, Ladson-Billings and *Rethinking Schools* keep these difficult issues in the conversations.

TOOL 2. HOME COMMUNICATION: LEARNING FROM FAMILIES

We require our teachers to arrange for ongoing communication with their student's family, and we offer a range of readings on possible ways to accomplish this (Compton-Lilly, 2003; Kyle, McIntyre, Miller, & Moore, 2002; Shockley, Michalove, & Allen, 1995; Spielman, 2001). The bottom line is that the family's lack of a phone, inaccessibility, or lack of response in no way constitute grounds for ceasing attempts to make contact. We require students to write a two-to-three-page initial agenda to accomplish this and to document their ongoing communication with, and learning from, the family, and how it informs their teaching. The ways in which the teachers communicate with families have evolved, and we offer several examples.

Photographs

At the beginning of each semester teachers purchase a disposable camera to locate, describe, and integrate their student's lived literacy practices into the literacy curriculum. In documenting lived literacies we ask teachers to explore not only book literacy but also the language, literacy, and symbols in the students' daily lives. These pictures can be used to build portraits of the students. Further, photographs help the teachers to better understand the children they are working with and the range of literacies that exist in the child's home and community. This documentation of lived literacies serves to spark a connection between the teachers and the students because the students see that their teachers care about and want to learn more about their social worlds outside of school. It also serves to broaden the teachers' notions of what counts as texts and literacy.

Family Stories

In *A Path to Follow,* Edwards and her colleagues (1999) document oral storytelling as a productive mode for communicating with parents, especially parents who may have limited skills with print. Consequently, family stories provide another means of connecting to lived literacies. One teacher invited family stories in the journal writing. Another teacher and her student brainstormed a list of questions for an interview with the student's grandmother. The teacher used this information as the basis for writing the following day. Another teacher sent a tape recorder home with her student and called the parents, explaining that she wanted the family members to tell a story about her student. She then transcribed the stories that served as the basis for a book about her student. Across the differences in approaches, the common thread is that family stories provide a text for the reading and writing curriculum. The themes important to the family and to the child become the text of the curriculum.

Family Journals

Family journals, developed by Shockley and her colleagues (1995), are a vehicle for communicating between home and school—an ongoing written dialogue. The conversations with the parents begin with the prompt, "Tell me about your child." The parents respond with detailed information about their children, including likes, dislikes, hobbies, and interests. These opening responses provide a portrait of the child and a space where the teacher can focus on the child's strengths and interests. In addition, there are many times when what is written in the journal also gives the teachers insights into the student's family and community.

The journals make it possible for the teacher to see the child as a person, often disrupting stereotypes and producing engaging relationships. Along with seeing the multiple literacies that exist in their lives, the children also learn that significant people in their lives read and write for meaningful, authentic purposes. One of these purposes turns out to be the family journals.

Observations of the Tutoring Session

Parents are invited to observe the teachers working with their children halfway through the semester for two reasons. First, it helps teachers to explain their instructional decisions to the parents in language that doesn't exclude parents from the process. Second, it helps parents to hear their child talked about from a framework of strengths and to see what their child can do when placed in instructional-level texts and engaged in learning activities designed for the child's success. One parent remarked, "This is the first time I have ever heard what my child does well." In addition to learning from the teachers, the teachers invite the parents to join in the conversations. During writing sessions, one mother helped her daughter provide more detail as she wrote a memoir about her grandfather. Together they talked about family adventures in great detail, which extended the daughter's writing. Sometimes parents reinforce their value and commitment to their children's education by asking siblings or other relatives to stop in and observe the session if they cannot be there. In one example, instead of the parent of the student observing the tutorial, the older sister came every day to the session 15 minutes before she walked her brother home.

Phone Conversations

Another way of connecting with parents is through phone conversations. Teachers use phone conversations in a variety of ways, but always to focus on the learning and never on behavioral issues. The teachers share information about the sessions and ask parents what they notice about their children as readers and writers. During these phone calls, parents often share insights and concerns about the children's instruction in school. For example, when one teacher noticed that her student wrote reluctantly during the session and shared this information with her student's mother, the teacher learned that the student had not yet experienced writing in her first-grade classroom, other than completing worksheets. Teachers also take the opportunity to elicit parent stories. Indeed, some parents call the teachers. Not all families prefer the phone conversations as their method of communicating with their child's teacher. However, if they did, we honored their requests for times that worked best for them.

E-Mail Conversations

Though many parents lack access to computers, some have access and engage with the teachers through e-mail. One grandmother pointed out that e-mails were the best form of communication for her, commenting,

> I turn on my computer every day, it's right there at home, I'm going to see it. Where, if I'm not thinking, I'll forget about the notebook, or he'll

give me the notebook early in the morning before it's time to come to school and I don't have time to respond. It's quicker when we respond to the e-mail.

Home Visits

Some teachers visit their student's family at home. Shireen, one of the first teachers to embrace the concept of home visits, wrote in her initial home and community agenda during the first days of class:

> I hope to be invited to visit Tasha at home. I am very comfortable with the idea and it is something that I did very regularly as a teacher overseas. I look forward to it but will leave it entirely up to Mrs. Parks—whether she has the time or the inclination to have me come over.

Shireen *was* invited to Tasha's house, and spent several hours talking with Mrs. Parks and visiting with Tasha. Tasha's excitement was evident the next time Shireen worked with her: "You came to my house. I loved it!" Teachers have picked up children (and returned them to their homes) when they have been kicked out of the after-school program well into the semester. Other teachers have attended birthday parties and church events with the children. Establishing contact with the families of students has the effect of changing stereotypes and breaking down fears of entering an unfamiliar neighborhood. As Kyle and her colleagues (2002) remind us, "Sometimes through visits we can learn information that can enable us to reach out to our students in unexpected ways" (p. 62).

The family literacy aspect of the program has even broader implications. Teachers notice the differences in family structure, with sisters, aunts, and grandparents as well as—or instead of—parents monitoring children's work or "staying on" (Compton-Lilly, 2003) children for academic achievement. They also come to understand the meaning of poverty: what it means to have no permanent phone or reliable transportation and to be unable to get an employer's permission to attend a child's school function. They learn what it means to care in spite of these obstacles. It becomes much harder for them to dismiss a parent's failure to attend a meeting as evidence of lack of caring. The teachers' developing understanding of home funds of knowledge (Moll, Amanti, Neff, & Gonzalez, 1992) is critical; only if the children's funds of knowledge are valued do they begin to count as cultural capital, and the teachers are the key to making this possible.

TOOL 3. MATCHING TEACHERS AND STUDENTS:
DISRUPTING AUTOMATIC PRACTICES

What appears to be a simple task of matching students with teachers is very deliberate, though it is more consequential for some teachers than for others since they have varying degrees of teaching experience. Course instructors match experienced teachers with students who are very different from their usual charges. The purpose is to disrupt automatic practices and, at the same time, to reduce the likelihood of hierarchical conversations in the group by rendering all of the teachers novices. Students in our program now range from grades 1 through 6 and are drawn from the after-school program (see the Appendix for more details). When we were located on the university campus, one of our teachers, Meghan, a kindergarten teacher, who was matched with a seventh-grader for the Lab experience, commented in her final reflective essay:

> I remember the day I was given the information about the child that I was going to teach (Julie). I was not happy, because she was a seventh grader and I was a kindergarten teacher. I didn't think I was going to learn anything that would help me in my classroom. Boy, was I wrong! I learned so much this semester, and I have taken a ton of knowledge back into my classroom. The best part is that all of this is natural now.

This strategy, while initially provoking some anxiety, makes possible more horizontal than vertical conversations among the teacher group because it reduces the significance of differences in years of teaching experience. It also makes it possible for teachers to ask for and give assistance, and to engage in collective problem-solving and what Mercer (2000) calls "exploratory talk."

TOOL 4. CRITICAL LITERACY EMPHASIS:
CONSIDERING TEXTUAL AND SOCIAL ANALYSIS

There have been steady, though not loud, calls for the need to move away from compensatory and remedial efforts to more critical approaches to literacy learning and social justice (Smyth, 2000). In light of these calls, in the summer of 2001 we introduced an explicit social justice component to the syllabus. While we believe many aspects of critical literacy were built into the program prior to adding this component (e.g., viewing literacy as intentional, noticing and theorizing about literate systems, noticing disjuncture), we had attached this to accelerating children's development as readers and writers but had not done so within a social, cultural, and political context. In other words, we were moving children forward as readers and writers but had not addressed the question, "Literacy for what?" We intended the new component to insist that teachers engage children in literate activities that are personally and socially relevant, to begin building critical literacy from the start, and to build literate practice with some short- or long-term implications of constructing a more just world. We provided three broadly constructed different entry points into critical literacy instruction. One was a genre approach (Cope & Kalantzus, 1993). A second was through student-led problem-posing, where the development of the literacy curriculum focused on the social issues of the child (Comber & Simpson, 2001). The third was a multiple-literacies approach where we encouraged teachers to explore, with their child, the multiple literacies that existed in their student's daily life (e.g., Pokémon and Yu-Gi-Oh! cards, electronic literacies and their accompanying guidebooks), and to capitalize on these during their instructional time (New London Group, 1996; Peyton-Young, 2001; Stevens, 2001). The different foci have raised different theoretical and pedagogical issues for class discussions (e.g., Rogers, in press). Each of the approaches to critical literacy are connected to social justice in the sense that social and textual analysis can lead to setting up the conditions of more just communities.

The idea was to open class discussions that would inquire into positive approaches to literacy in the context of social justice, thus potentially reversing some of the negative and passive expectations for these students. The emphasis on inquiry is important here as well as elsewhere in the class because, as Fennimore (2000) points out, "the presence of inquiry in the language of educators can support positive approaches to problems. When the language environment of a school is permeated with active inquiry, democratic questions about justice and fairness can evolve naturally" (pp. 26–27). For many this is the first time they have given consideration to social justice as a central aspect of literacy—aside from the general concept of equal opportunity in schooling. These conversations are often quite difficult, though ultimately worthwhile.

Jane's journal entry is representative of many entries we see as teachers develop their understandings of critical literacy:

> I wasn't really sure if I thought this critical literacy thing was a good idea, or that if it was, I thought it was making things more difficult . . .

At the beginning I was always trying to figure out what the heck to do with it . . . I think I needed to figure it out by myself. . . . If you had just told me and I had done it then it wouldn't have meant as much to me because I wouldn't have realized what an impact it had. [In the end,] I think critical literacy is what kept my student engaged.

Although many teachers follow their child's lead toward critically literate ends, the process of learning and teaching critical literacy is not without tensions, as the above quote suggests. Teachers want to know what *exactly* critical literacy is. Given that the underlying peda-gogical approach of critical literacy is not linear, we used inquiry in our efforts to explore the range of dimensions of critical literacy. Cen-tral to this approach are texts that are connected to children's lives and experiences, writing that provides a sense of agency, a sensitivity to patterns of language use, and an ability to adopt multiple perspectives. However, equally important in developing critical literacy is the abil-ity to feel comfortable with discomfort: understanding that important learning often begins by confronting issues we have learned to avoid. This turns out to be very difficult for most of the teachers we work with. One teacher in an early journal entry clearly stated this after reading an article titled "No Easy Road to Freedom" (Sweeney, 1997):

I would really like to do something like this, but racial issues are not the place to start for an untenured teacher. Also, I would be afraid to do anything controversial. I know that I should make literacy culturally rele-vant, but I really do prefer to avoid conflict. I just feel that there are enough terrible things happening in the world and I prefer not to dwell on the negative. I also prefer a peaceful existence since I have enough conflict in my own life. The children I work with have enough to worry about, as well. So many children have divorced or estranged parents. Others live in abusive homes. I really don't feel I should create any more conflict. This is probably not what you want to hear.

This tension does, however, lessen over the course of the semester. Another teacher who openly struggled with critical literacy, both at the lab site and in her primary classroom, commented at the end of the semester in her final essay:

Putting an idea out there for the class and just letting it take off is a scary thing to me. What happens if it goes in the wrong direction? What if someone says something that is offensive to someone else? These are things that I used to think. I am now more open about these critical con-versations that take place in my class. I have realized the importance of teaching a child to see the issue from all different angles—teaching them that they can make a difference if there is something that they do not agree with. I want my students to know that there will always be information out there to learn, that school is not the end of learning nor the only place that learning takes place. This reminds me of something that was said by Bomer and Bomer (2001), in the text *For a Better World*, "there is no single direction that everyone must go, and no one is ever finished with the journey" (p. 96). I am not so scared of this anymore and have seen the benefits in my [first-grade] classroom.

Our current readings include publications from *Rethinking Schools* that raise issues of gender, race, class, linguistic and cultural privilege, media, and sexual orientation. Examining the language in which the school is represented in newspaper reports is substantially easier than considering cultural privilege, not to mention sexual orientation in the context of religious diversity. The discomfort often leaves a nagging feeling among teachers that critical literacy is always about the negative aspects of society—a feeling that was heightened during the patriotic fervor of the invasion of Iraq. Discussions among these mostly untenured teachers at once make clear the function of tenure and the considerable fear that accompanies controversy. Fortunately, among each group there are at least a couple of teachers who try critical literacy teaching in their classrooms and report their experience in class, providing role models for the others. However, we still often find this aspect challenging, as it constantly raises questions about our roles and our rights and responsibilities as teachers ourselves.

We find it convenient when issues come directly out of the tutoring. For example, two different African American students responded to a conversation about Barbie dolls very differently—one had a collection, and the other referred to Barbies as "them skinny little stick things." On another occasion, after carefully selecting books at Rashad's level and remembering that his mother was about to have a baby, Hope introduced the text *Our Baby* (Bacon, 1997). Rashad responded that he didn't want to read about "black babies"—he wanted to read about animals. In another session, after Carla introduced *Just Us Women* (Caines, 1982), Janelle informed her that the book was not a good choice and she was not going to read it.

These discrepancies led to productive seminar discussion of personal versus cultural significance and institutionalized forms of oppression (e.g., racism, classism, and sexism) and how these play out in book preferences. Other topics, such as the Iraq war, death, and homosexuality, are far more difficult because of factors such as religious and political positions, and relatives in the armed forces. We see the difficulty our teachers have with discussing uncomfortable issues as a serious problem in a democracy, and as an important dimension of literacy. Some of our teachers are not easy to convince on this. The environment in which they work doesn't help. When the World Trade Center was attacked, the majority of the teachers were told by their administrators not to discuss it with their students. Consequently, when one of the fifth-grade students in the school was stabbed on the way home, the teachers did not know whether it was okay to talk about that with their student or, if so, how to do so. Multiple divergent newspaper reports of the incident provided one vehicle for addressing the issue. But there are many sensitive issues to address or not—parents in jail; a sibling, cousin, or baby niece murdered; and so forth—and, as Ilene Rutten, one of our instructors, posed it to a class: "What does our silence say?"

The next two chapters explore the experience of teachers who have participated in different versions of our classes. Both teachers reflect on their experience, specifically referencing the aspects of the class that were significant for them and how they transferred that learning into their teaching careers. Echoes of the tools we have described can be heard throughout these chapters. Both chapters clearly show the influence of the critical literacy emphasis. Chapter 5, written by Kim Prettyman, also shows her transfer of learning, particularly in writing and family literacy. Chapter 6, written by Karen Amundsen, opens with clear testimony about Tool 1, the location of the lab.

5

Rethinking Power: Learners as Teachers and Teachers as Learners

KIMBERLY PRETTYMAN

I went into the teaching profession because my first-grade teacher said she'd stand on her head when we were able to solve a particular problem. A few minutes later she was doing a handstand at the front of the class. That is just one example of the many ways she made us feel important each day, as a class and as individuals. It had been about that long—since first grade—since I had felt a teacher had made a personal investment in my learning when I came to the Literacy Lab. Although nobody stood on their head, I was treated as an individual and as an important member of a learning team. The Literacy Lab challenged my thinking about critical literacy, language choices, professional development, transfer of power, family connections, and classroom applications. But it confirmed what I have always known in my heart: Put the child first. In this chapter I will first offer my reflections on what I view as the significant features of my Literacy Lab experience, and then show how my learning transferred beyond the Lab to my classroom.

THE LAB EXPERIENCE

In a tutoring session we had 60 minutes to accelerate the child's reading, writing, and word knowledge, while taking running records and making detailed observation records. Initially, I felt inadequate. But with demonstration and reflective analysis, I learned. For example, my student quickly tired of my initial book introductions, which were long and detailed and previewed a vocabulary word or question from every page. Through observing his behaviors and lack of engagement, I realized I needed to alter the introductions to better meet his needs. My book introductions changed from being structured and scripted to interactive conversations as we walked down the hall to our tutoring location. I learned that Tekwan loved dogs, so I brought a book about a blind rescue dog to our next session. I shared some of the dog's adventures as we walked to our tutoring location.

As I got to know Tekwan as a person and a reader I chose books that he enjoyed, built upon his strengths, and provided practice for the skills he needed to work on. Our friendship grew, and I quickly learned about Tekwan's many interests. Through further conversations with his grandmother via journaling and e-mail, I learned more about him that guided my book selection and informed my instruction. *Matching Books to Readers* (Fountas & Pinnell, 1999) was very helpful for selecting books that fit his personal interest as well as instructional level.

I really liked Clay's quote of the teacher needing to find the "child's way to the teacher's goals" (Clay, 1993b). I learned in tutoring sessions to let go of the image of what I thought reading and writing behaviors *should* look like, and focused instead on what Tekwan needed them to look like. One of the most important lessons in tutoring and teaching reading and writing has been to be "flexible and let the child lead" (Clay, 1993). As I worked with Tekwan, I originally had my plans based solely around what I wanted to accomplish. I quickly learned how to understand what he needed and how he needed to accomplish this. By following the lead of the learner, we made progress. Tekwan liked to be the teacher, so we would often switch roles and I would ask questions so he could "teach" me about basketball or other topics we read about. We read and wrote around topics of his interest.

TRANSFER TO THE CLASSROOM

After our tutoring sessions, we were held accountable nightly, during the around-the-table discussions, to find the celebrations in our tutoring. This was a challenging task at first, yet it made finding the strengths of our students become automatic. Everyone had to respond, the responses were written down, and there was never an option not to participate. This accountability was crucial to my level of engagement and application, since I knew I was going to have to share a celebration each night and a transfer from the readings to my life.

WRITING

As my professors modeled with specific language what I was to do with my student, I applied this to my tutoring, which then transferred to my fifth-grade classroom. My fifth-graders became learners and teachers as well. They taught one another, me, and their parents as they explored these new learning spaces.

In order to foster quality writing, it is important for students to know why people write and what they can gain, besides a grade, from writing themselves. I have learned that students need choice, opportunities to write on demand, to know who the audience is, and to have a purpose in writing (Routman, 2000).

Three of my students currently hope to pursue careers in writing—one as a poet, another as a journalist, and the third as a cartoonist for Marvel Comics. The latter wrote to Marvel because of a business letter requirement and received a response saying his drawings were excellent, to keep it up, and to contact them when he turned 18. The student was so excited; when he shared his response with the class, all of the students saw that writing has meaningful, real-world purposes.

Conferring with students about their writing has historically been an uncomfortable space for me. In this course I learned to view writing as a conversation and to focus on the writer rather than the piece of writing. This was particularly reinforced through reading Anderson's (2000) *How's It Going?* Another helpful tool from this book was the conference sheet for documenting conferences with students, where I record the teaching points and praise points about each student's writing. I also acquired the concept of mentor texts from this and other readings: The idea that we can use particular texts as touchstones to guide our writing. I now view writing as always a work in progress, which my fifth-grade writers find liberating.

When my students share their writing, I ask them to take notes and borrow ideas from each other. Writing can be collaborative and is in response to what we notice in texts, in others' writing, and in the world around us (Anderson, 2000). But teaching, too, should come from what we notice in students' writing.

CRITICAL LITERACY

Critical literacy was introduced to me during the semester. When I first heard the term, I thought it was reading and answering higher-level thinking questions. Through the help of *Rethinking Classrooms* and

For a Better World (Bomer & Bomer, 2001) I learned that we can empower students to read and write for social action with the intended goal of changing the world. Teaching students to look critically at texts and the world around them can be fostered through reading and writing. Teachers need to ask the questions with the goal that the students will begin asking similar questions without prompting (Bomer & Bomer, 2001).

Book groups are one way I have found to engage students in critical conversations around texts. When discussing a book, I teach students that it is acceptable to disagree with one another in a respectful way. Previously when we held literature circle groups, the students took turns telling their part about the book, but the discussions weren't there. Now we dig deeper into the messages of the book, challenge the author, and begin asking questions during our conversations.

Teaching and learning critical literacy takes shape by asking questions, seeking answers, and taking action. When we ask our students to take action, we need to be ready to supply them with a realistic way to carry it out (Lewison et al., 2002). Writing for social action and justice provided a purpose and an audience for students who will then have reasons to develop writing further.

Responding to a Performance

One of the first ways my class and I began to look critically at the world around us followed a presentation sponsored by the Parent Teacher Organization of an adaptation of the traditional folktale *The Three Billy Goats Gruff*. This opera, about bullying and friendship, was intended to convey the message, "Kindness Is Contagious." However, the performers' actions during the entire performance did not reflect the intended message. Our reading and discussions during the Lab caused me to look at this play for what they were conveying inadvertently. The bully in this opera, portrayed by a large African American man, never attended school and misspelled a sign he wrote. The three victims in the opera were smaller Caucasians. The characters finally became friends when the smallest girl goat had the nerve to push the bully off the bridge into the river.

Immediately following the performance I wanted to hear my students' thoughts on the show. They thought the message was contradictory. They found the characters violent, even though at the end the characters said that kindness matters. We then discussed bullies—what they look like, sound like, and act like. Student responses ranged from *big, stupid, scary,* and *mean* to "anyone who is angry can be a bully." Following the prompt, "What did you think of the opera?" the fifth-graders discussed how bullying can stem from hurt feelings, anger, and loneliness. They also commented that the producers needed to be careful when they directed cast members.

I felt it was important to share this new perspective with the other teachers in my building. I typed a synopsis of the class discussion and challenged other colleagues to think about what messages were sent nonverbally to our students. When I shared a draft of my letter, Cheryl Dozier was helpful in choosing my language so that I would encourage my peers to think about this play from another perspective without offending. I received several positive comments in response and was encouraged by other conversations that followed with my colleagues.

Responding to Tragedy

Another example of children using writing for political action was after the *Columbia* tragedy. I wrote the following quote from *Poetry Matters* (Fletcher, 2002) on the board the day after the tragedy:

> Poetry Matters. At the most important moments, when everyone else is silent, poetry rises to speak. (p. xx)

My fifth-graders began discussing what the quote might mean and why it was important today. The discussion about the tragedy included disjointed details of the clips they heard from the news or their parents. After our conversation, we began writing poetry. Respect, patriotism, and bravery emerged in their poems. We all saw how poetry worked when words might otherwise fail us. The class created a book, which one of the parents forwarded to a state senator, who then forwarded it to the White House. The students received a response on White House stationery and were thrilled that their words had made an impact. When students have an opportunity to think and respond about the world around them, they are empowered.

TRANSFER OF POWER

Another critical component I incorporated into the class was creating social opportunities so the students were part of the decision-making process in the classroom. Transferring power to the students had several unintended consequences. I had hoped to increase motivation and student ownership of the classroom. That occurred along with many other positive results.

Teaching students how to communicate differences of opinions was a crucial component. *For a Better World* (Bomer & Bomer, 2001) helped me teach students language choices that were helpful and not hurtful in communicating their point of view. When difficulties arose, the students were part of the problem-solving process. Problem-solving moved from the textual to the social level. In one literature circle several of the members came to me saying another member wasn't participating. Instead of my usual response, telling the students what they should say and do, I began asking them questions. I asked the students what they had been discussing and if they had asked the other student's opinion. I also asked them what it must feel like for this other student, who was the only girl in the group. As they thought about the answers to some of these questions, their demeanor changed as they viewed the situation from another perspective. We all began to problem-solve together about ways to use language in the discussion that would give access to all members in the group. These conversations led to increased participation by everyone. The whole group felt as if they were part of the formerly nonparticipating student's success, as they had restructured conversations to include everyone.

The fifth-graders also addressed the class directly with their concerns, gathering information and congratulating others. They started a class newspaper in which they expressed their views, informed their peers of upcoming events and assignments, and published their writing. Giving students ownership of their classroom created a space to begin critical discussions, and to look critically at our reading and the world around us.

FAMILY CONNECTION

Establishing a family–home connection was another required component of the Lab. This mandatory assignment gave me confidence and strategies to access relationships with the parents of my own students I would have never believed possible. Over the course of the 3 years I taught fifth grade, this year was the closest I ever was to the parents.

Parent involvement changed in my classroom through the power of poetry. In the text *Rethinking Our Classrooms* (Bigelow et al., 1994), there was an article where students put their heritage and memories into poetic form. I enjoyed reading this article and decided to try it in my classroom. Using the mentor text, *Where I'm From* by George Ella Lyon, students followed the format to write their own *I Am From* poetry (Bigelow, Christensen, Karp, Miner, & Peterson, 2001). The very next day after the lesson, one of my students who is in special education came in with a poem he and his mom wrote together. After listening to this beautiful poem, we began to plan a poetry café and to consider how to get the rest of the parents in the class involved. The students were excited to write their poems. They had an authentic purpose and audience. Family poetry night was a huge success! The writing of the poems and the celebration strengthened the students' relationships with their parents, their peers, and me. It also strengthened my relationships with the parents. My mother, grandmother, and husband also wrote poems that were shared that evening as well. This was an activity and event that showed me that reading widely, reflecting, and implementing what is learned in a collaborative way make for astounding learning opportunities for the teacher, students, parents, colleagues, and others.

CONFIDENCE AND PROFESSIONAL DEVELOPMENT

If there is one outcome of this course that encompasses all the others, it is the confidence I have gained in myself as a professional. Before, if anyone questioned my practices, I questioned myself. If I felt my ability as a teacher was in question, I doubted myself. I did not view myself as the reflective scholar that I have become and still strive to develop further. I now know what I need to do to move students forward to develop a self-extending system, how I need to accomplish this, and how to articulate why I am implementing these practices with parents, peers, administrators, and other audiences. This course has given me access to language choices that help me to communicate what I know about my learners as individuals and how I plan to move them forward.

I have built a professional library and know which resources to refer to if I have questions in the areas of book leveling, word work, reading, or writing. Currently I am involved in a study group in my building based around the text *Words Their Way* (Bear, Invernizzi, & Johnston, 2003). Reading widely, starting and participating in other book studies, collaborating with other teachers, seeking out conferences and workshops, and sharing ideas with my peers will continue to be part of my professional development beyond this course.

The course not only caused me to rethink my current classroom practice; it has helped me to develop the courage and confidence to think about future professional plans. For the first time ever, I have begun to entertain furthering my education beyond this master's degree. I would not previously have considered this, but I have now had opportunities to share with or teach my colleagues in faculty meetings and districtwide grade-level meetings. These opportunities have increased my confidence and created a desire to be a teacher of teachers, a mentor, or a district Literacy Coordinator. My journey as a lifelong learner continues along with my students' in their journey. When I started this course I could not see myself beyond the walls of my fifth-grade classroom, and now many future professional possibilities beckon.

6

Teachers Teaching: Language and Power

Karen M. Amundsen

On the first day of class, I sat in a classroom with 13 other graduate students, arranged in a horseshoe, all staring a bit apprehensively at our professor. I spoke with my fellow classmates, who confessed to feeling a bit nervous about being white, middle-class women working with inner-city students. I felt that I had worked out my insecurities because I was already working in the school district where the Literacy Lab was being held. I spent the previous 3 years as a teacher's aide in a special education classroom at a middle school approximately 1 mile away from the lab school. My parents and sister were also educators in the same school district, and shared with me throughout my life their experiences about teaching in an inner-city school. As Becky, my Lab instructor, explained the content and structure of the Literacy Lab, I believe we all *thought* we had a fairly good idea of what we were in for in the 6 weeks that would follow. I did not realize how much I still had to unravel concerning the issues of teacher and student interactions: issues involving language and power that become more pronounced when cultural differences are included, issues that held the potential to break down or build relationships.

POWER AND LANGUAGE

I learned from my experience in the reading program that language is central to teaching and learning how to read. Language and power are part of literacy instruction through the linguistic choices of the teacher, the language of the child in accessing the written code, and the unstated assumptions in each layer of language. Because language is the key mediational tool in literacy teaching (Vygotsky, 1986) and it is always embedded in power relationships, it is necessary for us to consider how to address these power relationships in our instruction. Part of what we tried to do in the lab was arrange the learning so that the relationships centered on caring and trust rather than on control and power. At the same time, we tried to deal with power in other ways. For example, the teacher is normally seen as the "more knowledgeable other" in the learning situation, within an asymmetrical power relationship. This was sometimes the case. However, in the Literacy Lab I arranged authentic places where my student, Isaiah, was the more knowledgeable other, especially concerning his home and community.

Isaiah perceived himself as a "disabled" reader, a perception that initially was reinforced rather than undone by my actions and language. Despite hearing Isaiah sing songs and tell stories from home, I did not see that this was his way of expressing his ideas. I did not realize that he was very proficient at sharing his thoughts. I assumed that because he had struggled in writing within a classroom setting, he struggled to express himself. The activities that I had planned to accelerate Isaiah's literacy learning had nothing to do with his thinking; they centered primarily on words, not ideas. They were essentially fill-in-the-blank activities. My intention during these activities was to make him feel successful. I did not want him to feel like a failure by asking him to do too much. What I came to realize was that I was making him feel like a failure by expecting him to do too little. Isaiah helped me to examine many of my language choices because he listened to every word and was more than willing to point out any confusion that he experienced.

My expectations changed in part because of a chocolate chip cookie. One morning before Isaiah left for a field trip, I asked him to finish his cookie and describe the way it felt and tasted in his mouth as he ate it. He did this effortlessly and with great pride. He wrote, "My cookie is sweet and cholatey," with a big smile on his face while licking his lips. He proceeded, taking a bite, thinking and then writing, "It is sweet and salty." At that moment, we both realized Isaiah was a writer. With my new perception of his strengths, I prompted him for more and asked, "What else? Tell me more." Prior to this session my language had been dictated by my perception of his weakness, and my language choices revealed my expectations. I had expected very little from him, and that is what he had been giving.

When we began to explore issues and inquire into them together, Isaiah accelerated as a reader and writer. I needed to meet Isaiah where he was in his thinking. When this happened, Isaiah saw that the purpose for writing was to get ideas on paper. After this interaction, we no longer struggled for the position of power.

My language choices were often not clear to Isaiah. I was using the language that I had learned in my schooling and assumed that Isaiah would know what I was talking about because the words and meanings were so clear to me. Success came for both of us when we used a common language. Isaiah also struggled with the questions being turned back on him. In the beginning he often would turn the language back on me, using the same words I had used, as a way to put himself in the powerful or agentive position.

LANGUAGE WITH PARENTS

The role of language and power also comes through with the linguistic choices that we as teachers make to represent our students. Peter Johnston was my instructor for the prerequisite course to the Literacy Lab. He made an important point about language and power that has never left my mind. He explained that people sometimes use jargon to make themselves feel smart and to make others feel stupid. I believe one reason that I remember this point so clearly was that at the time I loved jargon and liked to use it as often as possible. It did make me feel smart. If I had gone through all the trouble to learn it, then I wanted to impress whoever I could with my newly acquired vocabulary. What I did not take into consideration was how it made others feel, and the channels of communication that jargon can cut off.

The carryover of "no jargon" to the classroom seemed a natural and necessary transition. Working with first- and second-graders, all language needed to be very explicit. Jargon would not have been useful in my goal to accelerate my students as readers and writers. Because I use explicit language with them, it makes sense to use the same language when I talk to their parents. Using a shared, explicit language helps us to avoid confusions and reinforce good practice. I was reminded of this again in my own classroom during a parents' night when I was speaking with a couple about having their child read easier "text" at home to promote "fluency." Luckily, the father said, "I don't get it, 'text'?" I apologized and explained that I was referring to books. He then asked about "fluency" and I explained that I simply meant reading at a speed that is similar to the speed of talking. His response was, "Oh, so you want him to read easy books, so he can read faster." His comment did not leave either one of us confused or in a position where we felt less or more knowledgeable than the other.

TRANSFERRING THE TOOLS

There were many powerful tools embedded in the Lab that I knew I wanted to apply as a teacher in my first job at a primarily white, suburban school. An inner-city school situation is very different from a primarily white, suburban one; so is transitioning from a one-on-one situation to a small group. We had learned about reading critically and I wondered what it would mean for students who live in the suburbs. I wondered whether asking students to read critically meant confronting them with everyday experiences of social justice, which would mean confronting what it means to be white. I wondered what their parents would think about their children having to confront their privilege. I reworked what I learned in the Literacy Lab to suit the context of a suburban school.

No longer a graduate student in the inner-city school with a multitude of multicultural materials at my fingertips, I was now a first-year teacher in a suburban school with an array of great books, but few books that could disrupt the thinking of my primarily white, middle-class first- and second-graders, few that by themselves could offer a different perspective into the lives of others. Or could they? Did critical literacy have to be about social justice, or would inquiry and critical analysis lead to this end by having the students examine and question all aspects of books? Was it the content of those books, or the way that the students examined the content? Just as I chose books that dealt with Isaiah's experience in the lab, I would be using books that dealt with my current students' experience.

I have to say that this was not some great epiphany I had as I stared at the shelves full of books with covers lacking in ethnic diversity. It truly came more out of necessity. The reading department was not scheduled to reorder until the end of winter, and trying to collect multiple copies of appropriately leveled, multicultural books for several class sections was more than I felt I could take on in addition to the stress of a new job. So I did what teachers have always done: I made do with what I had, and in that process realized that there is diversity in all aspects of people. Ethnic diversity is one that is often easy to see. Isaiah was ready to start his journey into inquiry where he was, as an African American male living in the inner city. My present students needed to start their journey exactly where they were, be it male or female, affluent or not. They could examine their experience in relation to others just as Isaiah had. Their inquiry would begin as Isaiah's had, where they were, through the language of inquiry that was used in the lab.

Prompting student thinking needed to be the starting place for instruction. I taught by asking students questions that allowed them to delve deeper into texts. They were questions such as "Why do you think the character did that?" and "How would you feel?" The students quickly got used to language consisting of questions they would ask of themselves and others. It seemed that whether in suburbia or the heart of the inner city, language was the tool that would propel readers forward. As the year progressed, the prompts, discussions, and inquiry came from the students much more than from me, as they questioned each other and the text. These questions propelled their thinking. They began to internalize my questions, and made statements beginning with "I wonder," and "I would feel." They began to interact with the text rather than just decoding words on a page. They began to expect inquiry of themselves and others.

When we began our independent reading of the *Triplet Trouble* series by Debbie Dadey and Marcia Thornton Jones (Dadey & Jones, 1997), Jay, a second-grader, looked over at me and asked, "Why do you think the author wrote this book?" I smiled, hoping I knew where he was going, and asked, "Why do *you* think he wrote it?" Jay said, "I bet he is a triplet." Cristin chimed in, "Or maybe he has triplet kids, because I probably wouldn't have written this book because I'm not a triplet; I would have written *Big Sister, Little Sister Trouble*. The best stuff to write about is stuff you know."

These types of interaction became everyday occurrences and were often student- rather than teacher-led, transforming the asymmetry of the power relationship. This language was also present in the response journals they used after independent reading. The "whys," "hows," and "I wonders," appeared on a regular basis in their entries.

It seemed that the process to prompt students to think critically was not so different in a suburban setting. It continued to be centered around language: mine to the students, theirs to themselves and others, and the language of the text. It also centered around an understanding that there were no wrong answers, only different perspectives. It was based on students reading against their own experience while trying to examine the experiences of others.

THE POWER OF DEBRIEFING

In the Lab we were given a half-hour after the tutoring session for "debriefing time." This was a period designated to reflect on the day's session and to "clean up" and analyze running records and other data collected. During this time I sat down and sorted through the details of the lesson, what Isaiah and I did and said, the moments when he was engaged and the moments when he shut down. Those periods of reflection were not always pleasant, and my list of what did not go well was often longer than my list of what went well. However, even on a day that was less than pleasant, if I had not taken a moment to unravel all the interactions that took place I would not have known what to do—or not to do—next. In those debriefing sessions, I used the language of my instructor to talk to myself and answer my own questions: *Why did I choose to do that? How did that go? Why do I think that worked? Why do I think that didn't work?* I supported myself when my colleagues or teachers were not there to support me. Just as debriefing was a useful tool for me in the lab, I knew that it would be beneficial for both my students and for me in a school setting.

My principal informed me of the class sections that I would be teaching and allowed me to arrange my own schedule based on the needs of the students and the classroom teachers' schedules. Scheduling was no easy task, with too many students and not enough time in the day. However, after several days of crumpling up papers, crossing out class sections, rewriting names, and starting from scratch, I had arrived at a final draft that seemed to satisfy the needs of the students, the needs of the teachers, and my own needs. I submitted a copy of my proposed schedule to my principle for final approval. By the end of the day the schedule was returned to my mailbox with a yellow sticky note that read, "Please see me, I have a question about your schedule," followed by my principal's signature.

My principal had called me in to say that before we could finalize the schedule we would have to make adjustments so that all my time could be accounted for, since I had scheduled 10-minute lapses between each class for debriefing time. Perhaps, in this situation, being a first-year reading teacher was an advantage because I was not familiar with the way others had done things before me. I was unaware that debriefing time generally was not included in others' schedules. I explained the schedule to my principal in detail. I used the term "debriefing," and that the 10-minute intervals would be used to analyze running records, record observations, and reflect on my practice, student strengths, what the students were using but confusing and a plan of action for the next day. I relayed my experiences from the Literacy Lab and my strong beliefs about the impact of this debriefing time on my instruction and my students' learning. Because our school employed guided reading techniques, I explained that this was the best way that I could meet the students exactly where they were and support student progress. My principal accepted my request for debriefing time.

TALKING WITH COLLEAGUES

At the very beginning of the lab, I only gave feedback in class if I was fairly sure I knew what I was talking about. As days passed, what began to happen was remarkable. A few of my fellow students began to take risks. They would share their confusions, issues, and celebrations with the entire group. As others, including me, began to see that no one judged these risk-takers, we all began to share. This sharing allowed us to learn from others' mistakes and breakthroughs. I quickly disregarded feeling foolish because this sharing was so much more productive and allowed me to realize that we were all in this together. Just as I viewed debriefing time as a tool I was not willing to part with, I also was not willing to stop using my colleagues as a resource.

Now, I often hear the language that Becky and Lisa, my course instructors, used in the lab to help me explore my practices coming from my lips as I talk to colleagues about their practices: *Why did you choose to do that? How did that go? Why do you think that worked? Why do you think that didn't work?* I have found this a useful way to use my colleagues as resources, and I believe that the feeling is mutual. Talking about our thought processes, our instruction, and the results of both helps me to understand why a practice is productive or nonproductive, and it also helps others to examine their own practice and the theory behind it.

7

Assessing and Representing Learning

In order to teach responsively, teachers must understand their students and bring substantial case knowledge to bear on instructional decisions. Our selection and timing of tools reflects this. The teachers are involved in problem-solving in every session, both through their own teaching and through their colleagues' teaching, and deliberate connections are made among cases. The idea is to stress the conceptual relationships among the cases, ideas, and experiences in order to provide multiple perspectives on each problem. At the same time, we are particularly concerned about the ways in which students, teachers, families, and literacy are represented. In their review of research on expert tutoring, Derry and Potts (1998) highlighted the importance of observing what students say and do—both the cognitive and affective aspects. For instruction to be fully responsive, the teacher must develop an understanding of how students understand what is going on. They argue that "during teaching, the expert teacher gathers evidence, forms relatively general impressions of the student, and then uses these impressions in deciding what kinds of teaching might work best" (p. 69), and that teachers do not construct detailed models of student knowledge. By contrast, the teachers in our class construct quite detailed models of their students' learning, including conceptual knowledge, processing strategies, students' interests, and the students' theorizing. Furthermore, they do this without using tests. This is also a focus during "roaming in the known" (Clay, 1993b), the beginning teaching sessions in which the teacher's job is to arrange for literate engagements in which the child can demonstrate (and build fluency in) the competence he or she already has.

TOOL 5. ROAMING IN THE KNOWN:
FOLLOWING THE LEARNER'S LEAD

Following the work of Clay (1993b), teachers are required to put teaching aside in the first sessions and, instead, arrange for students to be successfully independent with the literate skills and knowledge they already have. This is referred to in the literature as "roaming in the known" (Clay, 1993). While Clay's work particularly addresses first-graders, we extend her concept of roaming to include students of all ages enrolled in the Lab. This part of the program has multiple functions. First, it reduces the likelihood of teachers starting on material that is too difficult for the child, since a mismatch in difficulty cannot be masked by teaching over it. Second, it sets the conditions for teachers to see the students through positive behaviors—which in turn affects group discussions, reducing deficit-driven theorizing. As one teacher pointed out to the group when asked what she had learned after roaming in the known: "I learned how many strengths he does have. At first I thought, 'Oh wow! Do I have my work cut out for me!' Now I see all of the positive things." Third, it allows the teacher to locate the student's zones of proximal development without the use of a test and the effects testing can have on the instructional relationship (Johnston, 1997). Fourth, because the teachers are not allowed to teach, they are pushed toward listening and following the child's lead, which for some is very difficult indeed (Heshusius, 1995). Fifth, it temporarily interrupts common teaching/learning histories that the teachers bring to the interaction. In other words, roaming in the known insists on the development of the intersubjectivity necessary for responsive teaching (Grossen, 2000; Tharp, 1993).

During roaming in the known, the teachers select a variety of books representing a range of difficulty (e.g., Guided Reading levels B–G), based on student interest. We suggest that the teachers bring these books to their first session and ask their students to sort the books into three piles—one pile for books that are "easy," one pile of "just right" books, and another pile that is "hard" (Ohlhausen & Jepsen, 1992). This literate practice allows the teachers to observe what choice students make and how they view themselves as readers. Jennifer Grand, in Chapter 11, discusses this approach. Also during roaming in the known, students write and sample books within a supportive conversation so that a comfortable level of difficulty is located and a productive teaching–learning relationship is developed. Conversations around the students' writing provide a source of information about their knowledge of print conventions as well as about their personal interests.

Teachers find this to be a productive assessment practice, as Tina, a middle school teacher working with a fourth-grader in the Lab, observed in her reflective essay:

> Once I read Clay's guidebook I learned where to start with Isaac, as well as with my future students. The idea of "roaming in the known" was an idea that would change my teaching for the rest of my career. Before starting each school year, I would always panic and think, "What am I going to do?" I thought I would have to know what to do exactly with each student from day one. It never occurred to me to observe and to get to know each student's strengths. By doing this, I had a firm starting point.

Because we cannot separate what a child knows about literacy and language from the contexts in which it is learned, we ask our teachers to roam the community and familial known as well as the print known. Teachers take a range of approaches, including taking "print walks" (Orellana & Hernandez, 1999) with their students to document places of interest, asking the parents for photographs of their student when they were young (Allen et al., 2002), constructing a timeline of their student's life (Spielman, 2001), and providing a disposable camera for the student to take pictures of favorite people, objects, locations, or events to form a basis for writing. The purpose of each of these roaming tasks is to get to know the children and their family and community contexts, so that the teacher is better equipped to build from the stores of knowledge and resources the children bring with them to literacy instruction.

We believe, obviously, that "roaming in the known" also means roaming the values, experiences, strategies, and proficiencies the children bring from their homes and communities. We learn about what Heath (1983) called "ways with words" through supporting ongoing home–school connections that are also intended to foster connections and common support systems between home and school. These support systems can take several forms, ranging from more to less print-based. For example, some teachers started dialogue journals with their student's parents, and others "spoke" their daily messages and questions to the parents on a tape recorder—the parents did the same. The journals make it possible for the teacher to see the child as a person, often disrupting stereotypes. Indeed, as trust develops, many of the parents provide private phone numbers and e-mail addresses to the teachers. Roaming in the known is explored further by Lisa Strolin-Smith in chapter 8.

TOOL 6. DOCUMENTING LEARNING: OBSERVING LEARNING

Teachers are required to document and track students' learning through close analysis of various data sources, including running records (Clay, 1993a), students' responses to texts, student writing (Johnston, 1997), and associated word analysis. It is this documentation that makes it possible for the teachers to ground their discussions about the value and focus of their teaching. They cannot simply make assertions about students' progress, confusions, or difficulties without using warrants from the data to justify their assertions. This documentation becomes more refined as they become more attuned to the kinds of patterns to observe, through class discussions and through the course readings. Initially, documenting children's critical literacy and their writing development is quite difficult. The significance of changes in specificity is not lost on teachers. Mary, for example, reflected on the growth in her documentation of her student's learning in her final essay:

> When I was writing my final report, I started by reading through my initial assessment and updates and I could not believe how much detail I used in my last update compared to my initial assessment. In my initial assessment, I had included some quotes from Jalinda, but looking at my last update and seeing specific quotes from Jalinda, I realized how important it is to use clear examples and the student's own words. I learned more about Jalinda reading my last couple of updates than I did while reading my initial assessment, and it was because of how specific I have become and the clear examples I have been using. It was a wonderful experience for me to look through the initial assessment and updates to see how much I have grown as a teacher and as a learner.

Documentation provides a lever for helping teachers reexamine their instructional choices. Teachers collect evidence through their analysis of oral reading (e.g., pace, stamina, fluency, self-corrections, cueing systems used, etc.) in a range of genres. Evidence is also collected through documenting student responses to texts (e.g., media, print, drama, computers, etc.). Data are also collected through close analysis of students' writing in a range of genres and across time. Documentation helps to limit two tendencies: the tendency to rely on memory, and the tendency to only confirm hypotheses (Wood & Wood, 1996). As the semester goes on, teachers must specifically point to areas of growth in their student's data. For example, Table 7.1 shows samples of Kelly's documentation of Naquan's literacy growth over a 2-month period. The specificity of the data changes the group discussion and insists on representations that are more amenable to instruction. This detail also counters the tendency at the beginning of the semester to use global negative statements such as "He's a reluctant writer"—a discourse that parents also adopt. The language used in the

TABLE 7.1. Kelly's Documentation of Naquan's Literacy Development

NAQUAN HAS GROWN IN THE FOLLOWING AREAS:

Literate Practice and Knowledge of Literacy

- During the first sessions, Naquan made few connections or inferences about the text.

- Now Naquan makes connections/inferences, often unprompted. For example, when the text read: "Jack didn't move. He kept staring down at the floor," Naquan inferred, "He's really scared 'cause he didn't move."

- In the beginning, Naquan made connections to other texts with prompting.

- Now Naquan makes in-depth text-to-text connections regularly and often independently. When Naquan looked at a photograph of the Amazon River, he made the connection between how the photograph looked and what was written in the text, saying, "Oh, yeah 'cause they said they lookin' at the brown water in the book." He then returned to the text to prove his point.

Knowledge and Strategies for Text

- Initially, Naquan read an average of 617 words per session in guided reading levels G, H, and I (taken from the first two tutoring sessions).

- Now Naquan has increased stamina when reading more difficult text. For example, Naquan is reading an average of 594 words per session (taken from the last 4 tutoring sessions) in level L texts.

- While early in the semester Naquan cross-checked and self-corrected, he did not verbalize what he was doing. Now he verbalizes his cross-checking and confirms his attempts independently when solving the word parts.

- Now Naquan solves words by seeing little words in big words more independently. For example, he hesitated on the word "spear"; then, after solving the word, he reread to check and continue the flow of the text. When I asked Naquan how he solved that word, he said, "I saw *ear*."

assessment of students' literacy development is a central focus of the next instructional tool.

TOOL 7. WRITING REPORTS AND UPDATES: INFORMING STAKEHOLDERS

Our assessment procedure is for the teachers to involve their students in reading and writing activities that are within a manageable range (see "Roaming in the Known"), and to document what the child knows and does, as well as the circumstances under which he or she successfully does them. The idea is to inquire into students' literacy learning rather than to test it. While we recognize that the reality of assessment in school settings includes norm-referenced and standardized tests, we expect that teachers will gather assessment data within ongoing instructional interactions to find each child's zone of proximal development in reading, writing, and word work. The teachers may use standardized instruments like the *Diagnostic Survey* (Clay, 1993a), the *Qualitative Spelling Checklist* (Elbers & Streefland, 2000), or the *Spelling Inventory* (Bear et al., 2003), which provide direct indicators of conceptual and strategic development, but we emphasize that these instruments represent only one data point.

From our perspective, the assessment process involves noticing, identifying, and naming. It has consequences for subsequent language, interactions, and instructional practices (Fennimore, 2000; Johnston, 1992, 1997). The language of assessment carries with it social positions and symbolic power that can close—or open—many doors for children. It is because of the importance of this process of naming and classifying that we do not allow the use of norm-referenced testing and the discourse it brings with it. We also require that teachers not use jargon in their communication of students' development in order to expand the audience to include family members and other professionals. Teachers often find this requirement challenging. Not only is it giving up their professional shorthand, it means giving up a tool of power—a language they might use in, say, a Committee on Special Education meeting, when a school psychologist might retain the dominating language of testing. Ways to handle such situations are a topic of discussion and sometimes role-play.

We expect reports to emphasize what the child knows and can do independently and with defined support, and what he or she "uses but confuses" (Bear, 2000). Using but confusing is where the child has partial knowledge, for example when the child uses periods but not yet just at the end of sentences. These are all to be documented, with clear examples in accessible language. We provide guidance for the writing through a guide and a reading (Johnston, 1997). There are changes in the teachers' discourse across a number of dimensions. There is a shift in the ways children are described. Deficit descriptions are largely eliminated and replaced with more attention to what children can do independently, what they can do with assistance, what they use but confuse, and in what contexts. There is a shift away from trait-based descriptions, such as "laziness," to contextualized descriptions such as, "does not find *Nate the Great* [Sharmat, 1977, 1989] books engaging," including contextual qualifiers such as "when reading Guided Reading level J books, like *Nate the Great,* he has difficulty using the clues to solve the mystery."

The more personal, human representation of the child is the first section in all written reports. Teachers include background information about the child's interests, hobbies, likes and dislikes. Our goal in including this information is to help the teachers consider how the child's range of interests and experiences will inform the teacher's instruction. For example, in a written update, Tekwan's teacher wrote:

> Tekwan lives with his grandparents and his aunt. He is an enthusiastic student who enjoys all kinds of sports, especially basketball and baseball. He really likes practicing basketball and playing center field in baseball. Tekwan said, "When I grow up I want to be a basketball player." Grandma spends time with Tekwan reading at home. Through e-mails, she shared that Tekwan is also taking judo lessons at the YMCA and enjoys dancing. Tekwan also has a dog named Mystikal, a very important member of his family. His favorite foods include: brownies, pasta, and Grandma's goulash. He enjoys talking about his family and the trips they have taken to New York City. Tekwan often tells funny stories that connect to different books he reads. He has a contagious laugh!

The descriptions also come to focus more on what children know and can do and use but confuse, and on the strategic aspects of literacy, and they do so with more detail and with clearer and more focused examples. For example, consider the detail in the following example from Mary's final report:

> Jalinda questions the text if she doesn't understand what she has just read. After reading *Antarctic Seals* (GR Level: O) [Parker

& Parker, n.d.], Jalinda said she needed to go back and look at the food chain again, because, *"the author must have made a mistake, how could a Baleen Whale live off of krill and get that big?"* Jalinda makes text-to-life connections when prompted and independently. While reading *Antarctic Seals,* I prompted Jalinda to talk about what she was noticing in the pictures, *"Many of the seals remind me of fish, especially the leopard seal."* During a reading of *Through My Eyes* [Bridges, 1999] about the food Ruby's mother makes, Jalinda talked about the food her family makes and how the sweet potato pie Ruby Bridges' grandmother bakes is like the one *"my aunt makes,"* independently.

Jalinda takes time to think about critical questions. When asked how *The Hundred Penny Box* [Mathis, 1975] would be different if the characters were of a different race, she took some time and said, *"The people would talk different and they probably wouldn't keep a penny box, maybe they'd keep something else."* Jalinda is beginning to think critically about texts independently and is beginning to ask me critical questions. While reading *George and Martha* (GR Level: L) [Marshall, 1972], Jalinda asked, *"What [animal] would you have made George and Martha?"* Before reading *A Poke in the I* [Raschka & Janeczko, 2001] Jalinda looked at the Table of Contents and said, *"If I was the author I would have made the table of contents in lines because it is easier to read. How would you make it?"*

Although we have teachers write reports, they are centrally a vehicle for changing the discourse and the thinking that goes along with it. Indeed, the shifts in language over time, as the teachers progress in the course and tutoring, reflect changes in several other areas. First, the teachers have a greater awareness of the audience, that it might include a wide range of caregivers with a wide range of backgrounds and with a caring commitment to the student. This is reflected particularly in the ways teachers represent the students. Awareness of the effects of language, particularly professional jargon, on the readers leads to a reduction in the use of distancing and exclusionary language and clearer, more concrete instructional suggestions. Second, reports become more focused, with a clear use of illustrative examples, and reflect both a greater understanding of the students and changes in the teachers' understanding of literacy. The shift to a more contextualized view of literacy learning, without the negative-trait–like terms, reflects a new understanding of the teacher's and student's role in teaching and learning, representing a greater degree of agency on the part of the teacher in terms of learning context. More attention is paid, for example, to the kind of text or task demands under which students' behaviors occur.

The final report is written in two forms, a complete report (less than 8 double-spaced pages) and a "refrigerator sheet," which is a single-side summary sheet framed for posting on the refrigerator. We also expect teachers to provide concrete examples of teaching that could be used by the person reading the report. Copies of reports are made available to teachers as well as parents at the end of the semester.

In the next two chapters two teachers who participated in different versions of the class reflect on their experience, specifically referencing the aspects of the class that were significant for them and how they transferred that learning into their teaching careers. While both chapters show the traces of the instructional tools, Chapter 8, written by Lisa Strolin-Smith, focuses on the details of her experience in the Lab. She foregrounds the transformation of her understanding of family literacy and its relation to her student's learning. Chapter 9, written by Cheri Collisson, weaves together her Lab experience and her transfer of that experience to her current practice on several levels. Her chapter particularly shows the value of videotaping.

8

Beyond Print: Roaming in the Known

LISA STROLIN-SMITH

Most of my educational experience has been in schools and universities with other white students, taught by teachers who didn't expose me to thinking about cultural differences in ways that would challenge my thinking and influence my classroom practices. Living in a predominately white suburb of New York City, I attended neighborhood schools until middle school, when my family moved to upstate New York to another district that lacked diversity.

Attending a teaching college in Boston gave me my first experience with integration of beliefs and practices using multicultural literature in the classroom. After my undergraduate studies, I worked in a large urban school district in southern New York State as a special education teacher. However, obtaining my master's degree in Reading at the University at Albany was my first opportunity to develop the idea of using my students' primary discourse as the foundation for learning.

HELLO TEKWAN!

I was assigned to work with Tekwan, a 6-year-old African American boy entering first grade. I was nervous because I had never worked with an emerging reader and writer before. I quickly learned that Tekwan was a quick learner and risk-taker who would try anything. He made careful choices of books based on his interests.

While participating in the Literacy Lab, Tekwan made significant progress as an emergent reader using pictures to construct textual meaning in association with connections to his own world. His extensive vocabulary, shown in his oral stories about T-ball and his barbershop experiences, came from the rich language experiences he has had with his grandfather and grandmother (whom he calls Mom), with whom he lives.

In my initial assessment as a part of the course requirements, I reported that Tekwan knew a majority of his letters and sounds, scoring 41 points out of 52 on the letter identification test (Clay, 1993a). I characterized Tekwan as "beginning to become aware of print." In the initial assessment, I wrote,

> as an emergent reader Tekwan needs more positive experiences with print . . . Since he notices pictures support the meaning of text, I want to capitalize on this strength and continue by using a language experience approach.

I made conscious choices about each lesson that would honor his culture within purposeful literacy experiences. I also worked to balance power/knowledge relationships by building the curriculum around Tekwan's cultural and personal resources.

On the first days of class, I went with the rest of the teachers in the class on a "print walk" around the community (Orellana & Hernandez, 1999) to document the "lived literacies" that exist in the community—the literacy practices that children negotiate in their lives. Before I met Tekwan, I made several additional trips after class to photograph Tekwan's community. Using these photos, I wrote a book for him titled *Tekwan—Hello Tekwan!* and mailed it to his home before tutoring began.

Although I was excited about creating this book, in my initial home–school agenda I wrote: "Not having a set agenda about what to teach my families about literacy is a new viewpoint for me." My past connections with homes were mainly through a school-based approach in which we invited parents into parent–teacher conferences and sent home updates on student progress. This time my first encounter with Tekwan's family was through the book I made. In this book, I introduced myself with a picture and said that I was a student, just like he was, and would be at the elementary school on Wednesday. The book had pictures that corresponded to the text: one or two lines of print per page, and sight words that I thought Tekwan might read. It ended with a ☺ that said "I will see you soon." Tekwan immediately identified me when I went to pick him up from his classroom because of the photo I sent. When he read the book to me in our first meeting, he came across the first photo and shrieked with excitement, "Oh, my, that's where I live! That's my house! Hey that's my gate." He then

retold a detailed narrative about a barbeque that took place the previous weekend behind his gate. He described the firecrackers that were
lit, and their sound—"*ka-boom.*"

Tekwan's telling of this story revealed his clear understanding of
story structure and his extensive vocabulary. The photos allowed Tekwan to see a connection between home and school and to connect his
storytelling to his literacy learning. His primary discourse led the literacy lesson.

ROAMING IN THE KNOWN

Marie Clay (1993b) introduced the concept of roaming in the known,
in which, before beginning to teach, the teacher arranges for the student to engage successfully with print for several sessions to document
what the student knows about and can do with print, both independently and with a little support. It is part of Clay's (1993b) idea that
teaching requires the teacher to listen carefully before taking up her
side of the instructional conversation. Roaming in the known was central to our initial sessions. In my storytelling interactions with Tekwan, I was not only roaming in the known with regard to print, but
also with regard to Tekwan's home and community funds of knowledge.

During those first sessions, I noted that Tekwan loved to discuss
the illustrations in stories and that he had an advanced vocabulary.
After assessing Tekwan's concepts about print, I decided to build a
speech-to-print connection through the use of an alphabet book. Tekwan and I made an alphabet book called *Tekwan's ABC Book.* We used
a disposable camera and photographed each letter of the alphabet with
objects that he chose from throughout his school and home communities. This text allowed him to recognize each photograph and integrate
the word below the picture. For example, a picture of his gate represented the letter "g" and another of his house the letter "h." I wrote
the words "The Gate" and "The House" under each photo in the text.
During rereads and with prompting, Tekwan began matching the
words to the pictures. I wrote in my reflection,

> this information is the basis for my teaching decision to create
> an ABC book with Tekwan using pictures in his community,
> school, and home to represent each letter of the alphabet. I won-
> der if he would become more aware of the print if the images
> were ones that he came in contact with in his surroundings.

During roaming in the known, aside from noticing his vocabulary and story structure knowledge, I realized that Tekwan relied primarily on the semantic (meaning) cueing system, sometimes not using what he knew about grapho-phonic (letters and sounds) cues. I thought of my role as working within two interrelated zones of development. The first was complementing Tekwan's use of the semantic and syntactic (grammar) cueing systems toward integrating the use of grapho-phonic relations. The second was integrating Tekwan's cultural known—his family and community funds of knowledge and his knowledge of the cultural organization of the school.

INTEGRATING FAMILY STORIES IN THE LITERACY CURRICULUM

It was important for me as a teacher to establish a connection to Tekwan's grandparents, who also taught me about Tekwan and the funds of knowledge in his family. I listened carefully to Tekwan's grandmother to learn more about the family's values and knowledge. Through our initial conversation I felt we developed a trust and that I was being given the opportunity to be a co-teacher of her grandson. I sent a letter home to Tekwan's grandmother with the completed ABC book. This letter complimented Tekwan on his reading and asked her to share in his success by asking him to read it to her. The following evening in a phone conversation Tekwan's grandmother shared the events leading up to her guardianship of him, which I took as an indicator of considerable trust. At this time, I introduced the idea of sending home a tape recorder to capture conversations and stories about Tekwan shared by the many members of his family. My intention was to create a readable text with Tekwan that integrated his family experiences. This conversation had an enormous impact on me. I wrote in my family/community log: "I came to the realization that without the trust of a family one cannot possibly have a relationship and understanding of a community."

Shortly after this conversation, Tekwan brought in an envelope with several photos from home. I readily added these photos to the book we were creating from the stories Tekwan's grandmother was taping. Tekwan narrated each photo, proudly telling me the names and stories of each person. He came to a photo of himself in his red and white T-ball uniform and began to tell a story about how he won a trophy. Using this information, I planned the next lesson around a Reading Recovery level 3 text, titled *Tee-Ball*, by Barry Gordon. We read the text and then Tekwan told a story about playing T-ball:

In tee-ball you hold the bat with two hands.
In tee-ball you charge the bat and hit the ball.
You run to the base.
You have to put your foot on the base.
You have to run fast to the next base.
When you get home you go to the dugout.
You score a trophy!

By Tekwan

I recorded the story and used it as a basis for future texts for Tekwan to read. I wrote his words on sentence strips and asked Tekwan to reread each sentence to me. I then cut up the sentences and worked with Tekwan to reassemble the words in the sentence, reminding him of the meaning of the text he had originally constructed. I asked Tekwan to identify the initial sounds and other features of the words such as the length of the word, building his understanding of the concept of word. I continued to use the story as a reread with Tekwan, using a flashlight to highlight each word as he said it to reinforce one-to-one correspondence. This became a mentor text for Tekwan and he reread it many times, gaining confidence and fluency as a reader.

During a reread of his language experience story, Tekwan had a literacy breakthrough. He pointed with his fingers to the words as he read without prompting from me, demonstrating one-to-one correspondence for the first time. In fact, Tekwan read this text at the final celebration in front of his grandparents and other family members. Dressed in his maroon T-ball outfit and matching baseball cap, Tekwan read the story fluently and with confidence.

Next, we used the story *Grandma's Memories* by Virginia King (1983) (Guided Reading level F), as a shared reading to reinforce the importance of building literacy lessons around Tekwan's funds of knowledge. Tekwan was very engaged in the story and made connections to his life. These texts captured the importance of funds of knowledge in connection with accelerating Tekwan's strategic interactions with texts.

The recorded stories arrived, and soon after listening to them, I phoned Tekwan's grandmother to thank her for capturing the beautiful essence of their family. Tekwan's grandfather shared, "Tekwan means everything to me . . . he is my inspiration." His great-grandfather also recorded a story. His voice had a rhythm like a Southern jazz song, low and sweet. I felt honored that I was given such an intimate look into this family's life. In my reflective journal I wrote,

The emotion and connection I felt to the family after listening to Tekwan's grandfather say, "He is everything to me; he is my inspiration," was the catalyst for my future work connecting home literacies with school literacies. I used the funds of knowledge embedded in these stories as part of the literacy curriculum. This was the first time I felt assured that oral stories carried the ability to affect the lives of children deeply.

Tekwan's final language experience story was about his experiences at the barbershop. He shared the "Barbershop Story" during one of our last sessions together. He shared a photo of himself as a young boy having his first haircut. The language Tekwan used to describe the sounds in the barber's chair captures his imagination and narrative ways of knowing (Bruner, 1987; Heath, 1983).

The Barbershop (as told by Tekwan)
When you go into the Barbershop you sit in the brown barbershop chair with the handle on the side.

The Barber pulls on the handlebar and the chair goes up so he can see the top of your head with the lights.

The lights are so that he can see how much they have to do.

He puts a coat on you and it snaps on the back of your neck and it chokes, too!

He uses the clippers from the drawer and takes them and cuts my hair.

He scrapes up on my hair from the back. The clippers sounds like, "eeeeeeeee."

He takes the slapper and slaps the back of my neck, slap, slap, slap.

The barber puts grease on my neck and my head.

I get a lollipop.

He pulls the handlebar back and when I was a baby the guy helps me out but now at this age, I get up all by myself.

My Daddy pays the money to the Barbershop for thanking him to brush my hair.

Although it was difficult to capture the rhythm in which he told the story and the tone of the onomatopoeia that was included as he described the clippers and the slapping of the "slapper" on the back of his neck, the story speaks about the powerful experience of going to the barbershop. I carefully scribed Tekwan's words and then we reread it, reinforcing the importance of his stories and knowledge from his life beyond school. Tekwan's language experience stories exemplified his strengths as a literacy learner. His capacity to tell extended, descriptive narratives with awareness of his audience were ahead of his writing proficiencies.

I recorded and transcribed a total of six stories to make the book *Telling Stories About Tekwan.* Along with his grandparents, other extended family members also told stories about Tekwan. These stories helped me to understand the social organization of Tekwan's family and the roles of each of the family members. It also helped me to learn about Tekwan's learning outside of school activities so I could continue to build on his experiences and interests in the literacy curriculum.

I phoned Tekwan's home expressing my thanks, excitement, and appreciation for all of their hard work in recording these stories. For the first time, I clearly understood that oral stories can affect the lives of children deeply. Starting instruction using Tekwan's "ways with words" (Heath, 1983) and working from the known to the unknown provided a scaffold for him to use what he knew about language and the world to learn about printed literacy.

REFLECTIONS

Funds of knowledge (Moll et al., 1992) was the entry point that challenged my thinking about what "counts" toward becoming literate. Before the Literacy Lab, my white, middle-class ideologies about family literacy had never been challenged. This was the first experience I had with seeing firsthand how primary discourses can accelerate children as readers and writers. Moll, Amanti, Neff, and Gonzalez's (1992) work allowed me to embrace the learning of the whole child rather than the child as merely a student within the structure of a school. I worked to move beyond my prior belief system that insisted on a hierarchical power relationship as the teacher. By incorporating Tekwan's funds of knowledge into our time together, we learned together. We were both operating in our respective zones of proximal development. For both of us, the dynamics of traditional literacy learning shifted from knowledge being obtained and imposed by the school culture to an environment that accelerated learning because it was based on prior knowledge and cultural understanding.

Marie Clay's (1993b) philosophy of following the child's lead was a natural entry point toward the integration of the literacy lessons where Tekwan's cultural knowledge guided his emerging development as a reader and writer. I learned about Tekwan's funds of knowledge through stories and other artifacts of family knowledge. These provided the basis for his emerging literacy. Through this process I have learned ways: (a) to engage family funds of knowledge, (b) to construct productive circumstances so children and teachers can jointly propel learning forward, and (c) to document the way in which funds of knowledge can help accelerate literacy learning.

For me, finding a balance between the familiar (the classroom/schooled literacy) and the unfamiliar (the household/primary discourse) provided a powerful learning tool for my understanding of literacy. Indeed, in this case my use of Tekwan's language experience stories was one such entry point into this transformation of traditional schooled literacy. Using family stories was also a way to make student-created texts so that Tekwan could interact with stories that were important, meaningful, and relevant to the integration of his social and textual worlds. Tekwan began the summer tutoring sessions relying heavily on picture clues to support the meaning of text. He ended the semester looking more carefully at the words in print as he stood tall in his maroon uniform reading the *Tee-Ball* story he wrote.

I located Tekwan's "entry point" as a reader and a writer by moving from the "cultural known" and integrating it with the "cultural unknown." Looking at the zone of proximal development through a cultural lens extends the way the concept is usually applied in early literacy learning as a technical scaffolding of the learning of print concepts. My work with Tekwan did guide him through increasingly difficult concepts about print. At the same time, however, stressing the movement from the cultural known to the unknown helped Tekwan to strengthen his schooled literacy.

My traditional literacy curriculum changed as well so that it reflected Tekwan's cultural and linguistic resources. I believe that asserting the value of Tekwan's personal and cultural experience in the context of literacy builds a foundation for the development of critical literacy. It establishes his authority in literate interactions, positioning him as a knower with authority in our relationship. The similar positioning of his family and culture was no less important.

9

Teaching Children to Be Literate, Not Teaching Literacy

CHERI COLLISSON

Who do you teach? When have you ever been asked or answered that question? Probably never. More likely it was: *What* do you teach? That seemingly simple question is part of what is wrong with our educational system. We have been taught to think in terms of curriculum, not children. We need to bring the focus back to where it belongs—on the students. It became apparent to me that I had lost track of the reason I went into teaching—to help children—when I returned to the University at Albany to obtain my reading certification. I had been out of college for over 10 years and initially dreaded the thought of returning to school. What could they possibly teach me about teaching! I'd been doing it for 13-plus years, and quite well, I might add. I completely identified with Wilhelm (1997) when he wrote in his journal, "I'm cruising down the curricular highway, nailing lesson after lesson, skill after skill. I feel like a batter on a hitting streak" (p. 1). I, too, felt pretty smug about my teaching ability. I became quite an expert at *delivering* the fourth-grade curriculum. My students were meeting New York State's high standards, and all performed well on the English Language Arts assessments—well, almost all of them. There were always those few remedial reading students who struggled with language arts and the assessments. I wanted to learn how I could reach them, help them "fit into the program." However, after returning to Albany and taking two courses, I realized how little I knew about literacy education. I already had my master's degree in reading, a bachelor of science from another local college, and an associate's degree in Early Childhood Education from a different local college. I already knew how to teach the fourth-grade curriculum. I was now going to learn how to teach children who struggled with reading and writing. I realize this is a dilemma that many classroom teachers face: They are not educated to be their students' primary literacy teacher.

LESSONS LEARNED

The most important lesson I learned in the Literacy Lab was the power of individual instruction and the move to independence. As Lyons, Pinnell, and DeFord (Lyons et al., 1993) describe, "the difficulty of change I've come to realize not only is it hard for the system to change but individual teachers as well" (p. 196). The most difficult change for me was the move from being in constant control of the teaching as well as the learning: in other words, moving from "delivering" the curriculum to "constructing" the curriculum with my students. Lyons and her colleagues (1993) discuss the various roles teachers play during instruction. Sometimes teachers are active in sharing the problem-solving, but "sometimes they retreat to the neutral position of observer, asking the child to work independently. They shift their behavior as the student grows in understanding" (p. 85). This never became clearer to me than during my final weeks tutoring Nakresha in the Literacy Lab.

Nakresha was a 6-year-old girl attending second grade at Douglass Elementary School. Initially she described reading as "sounding out words, pointing to words, and looking at words." Near the end of our tutoring sessions Nakresha described reading in this way: "I just read, if I don't know a word I will skip it and go back to it. Stories should make sense you know." It was only after I started teaching Nakresha to *become strategic,* rather than trying to teach her strategies, that she accelerated as a reader. Skipping a word and going back to it was one of the more difficult strategic behaviors for Nakresha. When Nakresha was reading *The Wedding* (Cartwright, 1988) she initially skipped the word "dressed" in the sentence "We dressed up and walked around the room." She then went back to it, checking the illustration, and realized what word would make sense. I praised her success with this strategy and encouraged her to use it more often. She went from reading a Guided Reading level D text in September to reading a Guided Reading level I text (Fountas & Pinnell, 1996) at our last session in December.

Another resource that had a profound impact on my teaching was *Guided Reading* (Fountas & Pinnell, 1996), particularly the section on book introductions. The authors state: "The key to children's access to

the book is your introduction" (p. 136). Similarly, Clay (1993) discusses the power of book introductions. She says: "The teacher is en-
suring that the child has in his head the ideas and the language he
needs to produce when prompted in sequence by print cues. He
should know what the story is about before he reads it" (p. 1). This
became particularly clear when I introduced the text *Just Grandma and
Me* by Mercer Mayer (1983). It was a Guided Reading level I book,
the most challenging Nakresha read during our sessions together. I
began the introduction by talking to Nakresha about the time she
spends with her Nana. I asked, "What kinds of things do you do together?" I showed her the book *Just Grandma and Me* and asked if she
was familiar with the main character, Little Critter. She was. I said,
"Look where they are, one of your favorite places—the beach! Let's
look through to see what they do at the beach." We previewed the text,
discussing the illustrations and mentioning words that might cause
Nakresha difficulty, such as *umbrella* and *build*. I would draw Nakresha's attention to difficult words in a variety of ways. Sometimes I
would say the word and ask her to locate it in the text. Other times I
would ask her to scan the page and find any tricky words, which I
would then arrange for her to figure out. Also, I would show Nakresha
parts of a challenging word that she did know, like "old" in "cold."

Nakresha read *Just Grandma and Me* with support and made many
meaningful connections throughout the text. This was possible, in
large part, because I had chosen the book carefully and given a thorough introduction. I followed Nakresha's lead with a topic that was
relevant and engaging for her. Our introduction—which was really a
conversation about the text—helped Nakresha to be enthusiastic about
reading it, which contributed to her success. Wilhelm (2001) pointed
out that "the most powerful time to support reading is before students
begin to read" (p. 96).

Nakresha also helped me understand the importance and necessity of helping students develop a self-extending system. I thought
that was what I had been doing all along while tutoring, only to discover that I had encouraged Nakresha to depend too much on me. Prior
to watching my videotaped session, I had suspected I had allowed
Nakresha to become too dependent on me for support. I asked my
colleagues to observe our lesson and see if I was jumping in too
quickly. Each week, as part of our class, we would take turns videotaping ourselves and asking our peers to observe the tape. Prior to
viewing, each tutor would receive a brief narrative of what to look for.
After watching the tape we would comment on our observations and
make connections not only with our own experiences but also to the

texts we were reading as well. My videotaped session was one of the most powerful learning experiences I had. My peers shared both positive observations and suggestions. Almost all 12 noticed the same things. Among their comments were: I had taught Nakresha "an overreliance on one or two prompts," "Nakresha looks to you a lot," and "You help her often, don't you?" I wondered if I was allowing for enough balance between prompting and independence. I wanted to know if I gave her enough space and support to do the work of reading. After I watched the videotaped session twice I realized Nakresha appealed to me 58 times in one session. I knew I had to get out of the way and let Nakresha take on the work of reading. I felt guilty for wasting so much of our time together.

As teachers we are frequently told we need to do *more*. Well, I have learned, in a sense, to do less—less jumping in, less "helping," less controlling of both the teaching and the learning. This is truly a time when less is more. The results have been gratifying. Nakresha made rapid progress.

COLLABORATING AS A READING SPECIALIST

After completing my classes and obtaining my reading certification, I was fortunate enough to get a job as the reading specialist in the same district I had worked in as a classroom teacher. In this new position, my role with my colleagues changed as well. Currently, I am working closely with most of the teachers from third through fifth grades, a total of 12 teachers. I also confer with the other remedial reading teacher, the speech teacher, and two special education teachers. That brings the total to 16 peers with whom I collaborate regularly, a situation very similar to my experience in the Literacy Lab. In my previous role as a classroom teacher I had teamed with only one other fourth-grade teacher and shared materials with the other fourth-grade teacher. I met with the remedial reading teacher quarterly. That was the extent of collaboration. Now there is so much more of an opportunity to work across grade levels with a variety of people as a reading teacher. We have conversations about "our" students on a daily basis—usually informally. I understand the demands that are placed on both students and teacher in a classroom. My goal is to help the students experience success as readers and writers in the classroom. Together, the classroom teacher and I notice what works with a student and what doesn't. We offer each other valuable insights into the other's world. Just as when I worked with Nakresha in the Literacy Lab and shared

Nakresha's strengths with her teacher, I share the reading students' individual strengths and strategies with their classroom teachers. Although there are times when I'm considered a nuisance for "stealing" their students away, I think the teachers see me as an asset to them, their students, and their program.

THE STRUCTURE OF MY READING PROGRAM

As a reading teacher, my primary goals are to develop a self-extending system, promoting strategic reading behaviors among my students. I reach these goals by focusing on what I've learned from reading researchers and theorists such as Clay (1993b), Routman (2000), Fountas and Pinnell (1996), Wilhelm (1997, 2001), and Harvey (1998). My reading program emphasizes a) meeting the children where they are, b) introducing texts in an engaging way, c) having conversations about texts and writing pieces, and d) modeling.

When I began working with my 31 reading students I took both running records of their reading and gave independent reading inventories. I have color-coded folders for each grade level. Each grade had two folders. One folder held the students reading assessments (running records and independent reading inventories) and a record of each individual's choice of books for independent reading. I met with each student weekly and asked them to read aloud from their book and have a conversation about the characters, plot, and so on. All these data were continually updated. The other folder held writing samples covering a variety of genres. At the end of each marking period I would ask the student to choose their favorite piece and we would revise, edit, and produce a final copy that later went into their permanent reading folder. This information helped me to learn of my individual students' areas of strength and areas of need. I could then create a program that built upon their strengths. I am pleased to say that 14 students tested out of the program for next year. They applied strategies independently and work successfully on grade level now. Only one of my fourth-grade students scored a 2 on the English Language Arts assessment, not meeting the New York State standards.

Once I established what texts were appropriate for the students to do "the work of reading," I gave thorough introductions to the material. We preview the text for difficult or unusual vocabulary, have conversations about the illustrations, discuss the genre, and make predictions about what to expect. Next, I prompt the students to make connections between what they read and their own life. This is where the art of conversation can increase a student's comprehension. Through conversations I gain access to my students' prior experiences, both outside of school and with texts themselves. Nakresha helped me see the light in this area. She was always willing to talk about any and every text we read. I discovered more about her than I ever would have if I had just stuck to a question-and-answer session as I used to do in my fourth-grade classroom. I have had the same experiences with my small groups of reading students.

Prior to reading the text *Weather* by Seymour Simon (1993), I shared the photographs with the children. One student opened his eyes wide and exclaimed, "You mean we are on the outside of the earth? I thought we were inside. I thought if you tried to stick a pole in the ground it would fall right through." He had mistaken a lesson on the atmosphere to mean that the earth was not solid! Imagine if we had not had a discussion about the text prior to reading it. Perhaps that is one reason I feel closer to the students I work with now in remediation than I ever did to my classroom students. These children open up to me and share with me their uncertainties, their worries, and their celebrations. Our time together is flexible and safe.

Routman (2000) asserts, "Model everything—just because you've suggested a behavior or listed it as a guideline, do not expect students will do it. Every expected behavior needs to be modeled—often repeated" (p. 162). Recently, I was working with a group of 8- and 9-year-olds (notice I did not say third-graders!) teaching them about writing with details: specifically, using everyday words in an unusual way to bring the piece to life. I first read *Owl Moon* by Jane Yolen (1987), a wonderful example. Each week, I take 5 minutes to read aloud to my small groups. The texts I pick are chosen for a variety of reasons. They may support a nonfiction topic the students are learning about in class, offer exceptional examples of the genre of writing I'm teaching that week, or follow a particular student's interest.

HOME/SCHOOL CONNECTIONS

As a classroom teacher, in addition to teaching I was responsible for assigning homework, grading papers and tests, and completing report cards with grades and comments. Every behavioral issue that arose with 25 students had to be addressed. I was in the position of passing judgment on other people's children every day! As a remedial reading teacher, parents see me in a different light. Shockley et al. (1995) taught me a lot about developing *partnerships*, not *programs*. They state,

"Schools and parents have a shared and vested interest in children that almost demands some kind of collaboration. We believe, along with an increasing number of home and school educators that this shared responsibility should be a genuine partnership" (p. 91). I have certainly experienced that with the remedial students I work with. I work hard to keep communications open between the families of the children I serve and myself.

In September I send home a letter introducing myself; later in the fall I participate in both afternoon and evening parent–teacher conferences; and at the end of each semester I send home a letter informing parents of the skills covered and texts read. I also include information about assessments given with general comments regarding effort and participation. I celebrate their children's successes. I share the strategies that the students are learning and the titles of the texts the students are choosing. I also include my e-mail address and phone number if they have any questions or concerns. Being a parent of my own two school-age boys has helped me empathize with the parents of the children. I have learned the importance of the students' lives and literary experiences outside of school. It is my responsibility to provide as many avenues for communication as possible to maintain the connection between home and school.

FUTURE GOALS

At the end of the school year I like to reflect on what worked well and what could be improved. At this point, I would like to individualize my reading instruction more. As Clay (1993b) states, "What is difficult about reading differs markedly from child to child. The programmes they have been placed in have been prescriptive and general" (p. 7). While trying to provide a balanced approach offering multiple opportunities to do the work of reading, I continue to struggle with difficult tensions. For example, in my work I try to meet the children where they are while at the same time helping them navigate the difficult texts they are expected to read in their regular classrooms. I want to continue to provide the reading text that offers the right level of support and challenge for their current competence. I agree with Regie Routman's ideas on the practice factor. Routman (2000) observes that "Kids will not become readers without massive amounts of experience reading independently, both at school and at home" (p. 111).

I want to continue guiding students in choosing books of appropriate difficulty for outside reading. Many of my students have trouble with this, choosing books that are too hard. I use what Harvey (1998) calls the "Goldilocks Approach"—finding books that are neither too hard nor too easy, but just right! We have spent a great deal of time learning to do just that this year.

I look forward to making improvements to next year's program and the years to come after that. Because it was my first year as a reading specialist in a different school, I kept a journal of sorts filled with practical and reflective pieces. On the practical side I wrote down the names of the teachers I would be working with, their grade, and their students. It was here I also recorded their preferences (push-in or pull-out, morning or afternoon, etc.). I also made notes to myself of things to remember for the following year and filed them in folders labeled by the month. Reflecting on what worked and what didn't was useful as well. I'm constantly thinking, *How could I have done that better—smarter?* Because I'll be working with many of the same students next year, I feel I have a head start over last year. I have records of the kinds of books each child is interested in, their current reading level, strengths and areas of need. I've developed relationships with their parents. Thinking about instruction and what drives my instruction is an ongoing process and will help improve my teaching each year. I am combining my passion for literacy with my passion for teaching: children, not curriculum.

10

Building Learning Communities

Preparing socially responsible teachers involves creating a learning environment in which teachers learn how to construct and use learning communities to expand their own learning, perspectives, and problem-solving. For this to happen, we have to build foundations of trust and respect, and a willingness to engage with the learning events. Although we present these conversations as tool 8, they are really the foundation for many of the other tools. We follow this with description of a tool that contributes to these conversations—teachers' responses to the course readings (tool 9). We think of this as bringing together the local professional community of the class and the larger professional community of teachers and other researchers. Tool 10 is the final celebratory performances of the students for their families, which is an expansion of the nightly celebrations of learning in the community conversations. The last tool in this chapter, tool 11, is the reflective essay teachers write at the end of the course. This is the conscious examination of the internalized learning conversations from the class.

TOOL 8. INSTRUCTIONAL CONVERSATIONS: DEVELOPING A COMMUNITY OF LEARNERS

Community-building begins even before the start of the semester with a letter sent from the instructor to each teacher enrolled in the lab. In this letter, we ask that the teachers send an e-mail discussing their teaching experiences, future plans, and what topics they would like addressed during the seminar portion of the class. Our final question—"What should we know about you that will help us make this a rewarding learning experience for you?"—is designed to support our responsive teaching. We use the information gained from these e-mails to welcome our students and to plan the first few nights of the course.

In the letter we also ask that the teachers bring artifacts to introduce themselves on the first night. We provide name plates for everyone and insist that the teachers refer to each other by name (and when they start tutoring, refer to their student by name as well) during all class conversations. The first class session opens with "What are your burning questions?" Once the teachers' questions have been addressed, we move to introductions, a discussion of the syllabus, and the instructional events for the session. We make it clear from the first moments of class that we will talk and reason together in this learning space.

Conversations are a pivotal tool in the course, and we want to organize conversations that will be informed and will be reflected in members' thinking. The conversations in the class are structured so that teachers will take an active and productive role in their learning and that of their colleagues. In the conversations teachers are required to emphasize the positive and productive aspects in the behaviors of their students, their colleagues, and themselves. The conversations encourage connection-building, including between and within cases, between student instruction and research, and between student and teacher learning and instruction. The conversations are also intended to encourage theorizing with accompanying warrants—supporting evidence—and reflection on content and process.

Another aspect of the community-building is providing food for each session. Food is necessary both because of the timing of the classes (4:00–7:00, falling for most after a day of teaching), and because sharing food provides another place for connection among teachers. A sign-up sheet at the beginning of the semester organizes this.

The group analytical "around-the-table" conversations are structured to ensure participation by all teachers in small- (3–4) and large-group sessions. These group conversations are intended to produce a situation of shared cognition or exploratory talk (Mercer, 2000) such that the group itself is able to produce what Mercer calls an "intermental development zone" (IDZ): a more social take on the individual zone of proximal development, a location for collaborative thinking. To this end, these conversations involve a deliberately shifting and diminishing support system on the part of the instructor. They are intended to produce in teachers both the expectation of such professional conversations and the capability of producing them. Consequently, the nature of these conversations is also the object of discussion along the way.

Not just any conversation will produce a productive intermental zone. We have to establish what Mercer (2000, p. 173) calls "exploratory talk," in which participants are centrally concerned with a common goal of "jointly and rationally making sense" rather than with "protecting their separate identities and interests." Exploratory talk is characterized by a tentativeness—the offering of unfinished ideas with the expectation that others might pick them up and extend them—and by explicit explanations and collaborative elaborations. Such talk requires that participants share a common goal of an "improvable object": an idea, solution, or practice (Hume, 2001; Wells, 2001) that is jointly constructed. This aspect of the conversation is evident in Mary's final essay comments:

> Although I am sad to see the course end, I am glad I had the opportunity to work with people who helped me to realize I am not alone when I struggle with a part of my lesson. Almost everyone has been there before and is willing to share their ideas and insights. I think no matter how bad any of the sessions were, we all knew we were not alone and everyone was honest. No one pretended they had the perfect session every time and everyone was willing to give suggestions, which helped me a lot.

Such conversations require that participants understand that when they put forward an idea or suggestion, no matter how tentative or potentially problematic, it will be taken seriously as a thoughtful offering, and perhaps extended. If rejected, it will be with an explanation that does not devalue the contribution or, especially, the contributor. This sort of talk cannot happen without a trusting relationship among the community members and an appreciation for the value of difference for opening new possibilities. These features are necessary, since participants must stretch beyond what they are already comfortable with so that collectively they can produce something that individually they could not.

These around-the-table conversations are particularly important in organizing the overall experience of the teachers. For example, Stacie observed in her final reflective paper:

> I came into this class with the notion that my lack of experience with children would put me to a great disadvantage. I felt somewhat intimidated because I have never taught and most of the others in our class have had a lot of experience in the classroom. What I eventually learned was that we were all "in the same boat" . . . instead of feeling inferior, I soon realized that the expe-

rience each person brought into our classroom would better prepare me for what I might face in the future. The interaction with
each one of my colleagues would give me the benefit of their experience. Listening to their day-to-day struggles and triumphs
was just as valuable as the material we were reading and discussing each class session.

Her reflection captures some important aspects of this complex
"learning space"—the safety and the nonhierarchical structure, the latter of which is achieved against the initial beliefs of most of the teachers. For example, in some semesters we have documented it is common for *all* questions from the teachers to initially be directed to the
instructors. By midway through the semester instructors are included
primarily as other participants in the group (Johnston, Dozier, &
Grand, 2000).

Several actions are responsible for this shift in positioning in the
group. First, the instructors turn questions back to the group, saying,
for example: What do you think? We just saw one way into the text,
what are some others? Talk about what you just saw. Second, they
turn attention back to available data, readings, or other teachers' experience. For example, if a connection can be found to a productive practice in another teacher's session, that teacher is asked to explain what
happened as a vehicle for problem-solving. This identifies teachers as
knowledgeable others, giving credibility to their teaching experience
as a source of problem solving. Third, problem-solving is normalized.
It is expected that everyone will be working on problems with their
teaching. Fourth, what is consistent across the conversations at all levels is the central emphasis on what is going well and on the process of
problem identification and multiple possible solutions. This reflective
conversation is central to the process of developing strategic teachers
by developing, as Wells (2001, p. 193) puts it,

> a "meta" stance to the procedures involved in the inquiries and to the
> strategies that different individuals and groups have used to solve the
> problems they encountered. By making these matters explicit, there is an
> opportunity . . . to learn about procedures and strategies of which they
> may not be aware and to add them to the tool kit of resources from which
> they can choose according to the demands of the particular tasks in which
> they are involved.

Though Wells is describing the process for children, it is exactly
the process for the adult teachers. It is part of the development of a
way of talking and representing teaching and learning that is self-
extending.

TOOL 9. RESPONDING TO BOOKS AND ARTICLES:
CONNECTING THEORY AND PRACTICE

Teachers write responses to the readings assigned for each session. Some of the readings are read by all class members and some are selected from themed options. The journal responses are designed with two major purposes. The first is to connect each teacher's practice with the larger world of professional practice and research. The second is to use the responses as a basis for conversations in and outside of our program, creating a reflective teaching lens. Teachers' reactions to and records of the readings form a textual background to the community conversations. The responses to the readings are drawn on explicitly, for example, when teachers do their reflective teaching journals, in postobservation debriefing sessions, and during conversations around the videotapes (see Chapter 12). The readings are selected to provide instructional examples, cases, and theoretical frameworks, and to raise issues for and to inform discussion. We ask that these responses not be summaries, but rather responses to the readings, raising questions and considering applications and connections to teaching practice and experience.

Teachers do not shy from difficult issues in these journals, often questioning the readings. Of course, some of the readings are selected to encourage questioning. For example, they read much Reading Recovery–related material, in which teachers are required to be highly trained. However, they also read Juel's (1996) study using college athletes to tutor children. These views of intervention offer conflicting views of how much education is needed for teachers of students experiencing difficulty becoming literate. It forces them to consider the trade-offs and when different options might be appropriate. Articles like Schneider's (2001) "No Blood, Guns or Gays Allowed! The Silencing of the Elementary Writer" also provoke discussion of difficult instructional dilemmas.

Even at the beginning of the semester some of the teachers take a critical stance. For example, having read and responded to *The Dreamkeepers* (Ladson-Billings, 1994) before the first class, Laura had the following comments.

> I just got the impression as I read the first chapter of *Dreamkeepers* that the author was blaming the teacher for the ways the schools are run and the performance of the students. I took it personally that she was telling me as a white teacher in an inner city with mostly African American children that I was not doing a good

job and that I was not treating my students with the respect that they deserve. I also happen to teach in a magnet school that Ladson-Billings says uses "desegregation money" to offer special programs, and yet we are still putting the African American students in lower level classes.

In chapter 3 I found Ladson-Billings' discussion of the students' skin color to be interesting. When I first read a passage on page 33 that stated that if we are dismissing the color of students' skin that we are ignoring the most important thing about them, I initially did not agree with this statement. But as I re-read it I decided that what she stated was true, and that we should not ignore the color of a student's skin, but take it into consideration when we are planning for our classrooms.

Mary, too, wrote about her conflicting thoughts while reading *The Dreamkeepers.* Mary's comments focused on her experiences as a white woman teaching African American children and her attempts to remedy the disjunctures that she noticed the students experienced when they were not provided with culturally relevant materials.

After I finished reading *The Dreamkeepers* by Gloria Ladson-Billings, I took some time to reflect on what I had learned from the book. *The Dreamkeepers* made me think back to the tutoring experience I had with the America Reads program. During my time as an America Reads tutor, I worked with two students for 1 hour, 3 days a week. The elementary school where I tutored was in a school district made up of mostly lower middle class students. Although the school population was primarily white, the majority of the students to be tutored were African American. The volunteer tutors selected for this school were all Caucasian.

I think I went back to this experience because the tutors chosen for this particular elementary school had very little in common with the students we were working with, which is one of the main ideas Ladson-Billings discusses in her book. I worked with two African American students. The reading teacher in the school, our supervisor, gave us books to read with our students about families made up of a mother, father, and two children. These books were not reality to almost all of the students that we were working with, but they were all we had. Many of the tutors, myself included, began making books with our students about their lives and their families, celebrating their individuality (something I don't think they were given much opportunity to do in school).

I think this experience came to mind after reading *The Dreamkeepers* because it is one example of how we need to rethink the way we teach children from diverse backgrounds. Gloria Ladson-Billings talks about "culturally relevant teaching" which allows students to choose academic excellence yet still identify with their culture (p. 17). The big question I kept coming back to while reading *The Dreamkeepers* and one I want to work through during my tutoring experience this semester is, how can I practice culturally relevant methods of teaching? One of the best ways for me to start is to believe in all the students I teach and believe that all of my students are capable of succeeding. After reading *The Dreamkeepers*, I realize how important it is to make connections to students' lives and to let our students know that their lives are important to us. I want my students to know that I will do everything possible to help them reach their goals—after all that is what being a teacher is all about, setting our students up for success.

Many of the readings for the course are chosen to produce these tensions. The instructor's job is to focus attention on the disjunctures to produce theorizing and conceptual change—to keep teachers in their intellectual development zones. As the above examples suggest, teachers are in their zones with respect to matters of race and privilege as much as with matters of teaching and learning.

While the above examples highlighted conflicts experienced while responding to course readings, we also see in the following journal responses examples of leadership and transfer beyond the lab. In the first of the two examples, Marissa discusses how her rereading of Clay's *An Observation Survey* (1993a) transfers to her kindergarten teaching outside of the course.

> *Observation Survey*, Marie Clay, Chapters 1–3. I have read this text several times, however I took another look at it to refresh my understanding of the content. I can relate to many of the topics that were discussed as a kindergarten teacher. I observe students who are just starting school, and I know how important it is to be aware of their emerging literacy. Some students come to my class with a great deal of knowledge about letters, sounds, words, letters, concepts of print, etc. while others come to school with very little knowledge about these concepts. However, many

of them have literacy knowledge that they do not recognize, such
as the ability to read signs and know how to find their name.

Some portions of the text made me think about my own
teaching strategies, and gave me ideas for improvement. Now
that we are halfway through the school year, some of my students are reading, and I am now thinking of ways to help them
monitor their own reading and cross-check the three cueing systems. I also started to think about the students that I have this
year, and how they are so different from each other. As I stated
before, some of my students came to school with a great deal of
knowledge and moved ahead quickly, while others moved much
slower. On the other hand, some of my students came to class
and seemed to have very little literacy background, however,
once they began to be immersed in print they took off very fast.
Every student learns at their own pace, in their own way. As
Clay discussed in the text, we must look at what individual students know and how they learn best. I believe that this is what
helps us to give students the types of opportunities to accelerate.

The next example includes a segment from Marissa's response to
the text *Reaching Out* (Kyle et al., 2002). In this response, Marissa de-
scribes how the readings inspired her to consider the issues involved in
planning and organizing family workshops with the goal of sharing this
information with her school colleagues. Indeed, Marissa did take on a
leadership role by presenting a plan to her faculty and developing family literacy workshops for her building for the following school year.

Reaching Out, by Kyle, McIntyre. The authors discussed family
workshops, and how they get families involved in the classroom.
I really like the ideas they had, and will be discussing this type
of activity with the other teachers I work with. I would like to
incorporate these types of experiences into my school. I can see
how the parents, students, and teachers could learn a tremendous amount from this type of interaction. The authors mentioned that these activities build partnerships, and help to show
parents that the school is theirs!

I feel that the teacher would have to give clear directions
about what the workshop would include. This would mean that
you would have to think very carefully about the families that
you have, and make sure that they would feel comfortable with
the activities. For the class that I have now, I would need some
interpreters for non-English speaking families, and would need

to provide some type of daycare for younger siblings. I have several families who have five or six children, and most of them are younger than my students. I think that I would begin with a literacy workshop to show parents how easy it can be to get involved in the process of teaching their child to read. I believe that this would be a great opportunity to model how to work through a book with parents, or other family members.

Each semester the readings are updated based on the latest publications and student reactions to the different articles, and it is often surprising how different sections of the class respond to different readings. The readings and topics are chosen for very specific reasons. Because we expect and encourage these teachers to become leaders in their buildings in the domain of literacy, we require them to have a substantial professional library. Teachers routinely share books and articles with colleagues and begin discussion groups. There are foundation books that provide resources for the relevant theory and practice (e.g., Clay, 1993b; Routman, 2000), including books on word knowledge (e.g., Bear, 2000; Pinnell & Fountas, 1998), different aspects of writing (e.g., Anderson, 2000; Graves, 1989), and book choice (Braus & Geidel, 2000; Fountas & Pinnell, 1999; Pinnell & Fountas, 2001). (In chapter 14 Vanessa la Raé expands the topic of book choice in this context and beyond.) We also require teachers to read one of a selection of books on connecting with families, particularly those including cultural issues (e.g., Compton-Lilly, 2003; Kyle et al., 2002; Shockley et al., 1995), and on race/culture issues (e.g., Ladson-Billings, 1994). Critical literacy is addressed through articles and books (e.g., Bigelow et al., 1994; Bigelow, Christensen, Karp, Miner, & Peterson, 2001; Bomer & Bomer, 2001). Often, because we have offered a choice of resources, discrepancies between the theoretical foundations of two books produce useful discussions.

These books are supplemented by a range of articles on electronic reserve with related themes, including the following topics:

- *Contextualized case studies*, particularly case studies of children who encounter difficulties in literacy development for different reasons (e.g., Glasswell, Parr, & McNaughton, 2003; Moll, Saez, & Dworin, 2001). These cases are selected for the ways in which they raise questions about current practice and provoke contextualized theorizing about children's literacy difficulties.
- *Critical literacy*. Accessible, practical articles are most important (e.g., Lewison et al., 2002; Simpson, 1996).
- *Educational theorizing*. We select accessible articles that either di-

rectly address the theory underlying practice (e.g., Schwartz, 1997) or provoke teachers to theorize about their practice (e.g., Commeyras, 1994).

- *Institutional issues.* Articles we choose for this topic critique current roles and institutional practices and offer alternative options (Allington, 1994; Brandts, 1999).
- *Media literacy.* Increasingly we find disparities among the teachers in their sophistication with electronic literacies. Although we have assignments that demand the use of such literacies, articles address the bigger picture, particularly showing where we are in the development of electronic literacy, and offering the necessary imaginative possibilities for responses (e.g., Coiro, 2003; Smolin, 2003).

In general, we look for articles that help organize thinking, produce critical discussion, show concrete examples of classroom teachers contemplating and changing their practice, and invite exploration of the disjunctures in theory and practice. We also supplement the readings with Web site addresses and Internet searches (including IRA and NCTE position statements), and we encourage teachers to bring in examples of interesting sites as well. The problem we routinely struggle with is the need to drop papers when we add new ones. There is a real tension between the amount of reading and teachers' ability to read particular studies thoroughly and critically. However, the library e-reserve allows us to maintain access to previous readings for students wishing or needing to pursue particular topics.

As instructors, we respond after each session to what the teachers have written in their journals. Our responses are designed to celebrate connections as well as nudge the teachers to consider a more in-depth or broader analysis of the readings. Typical responses include "Important consideration," "Nice connection to earlier readings in the course," "How does this point connect to your earlier responses?," "What other ways have you considered?," "How does this point connect to your work with ____?," "To consider." Our responses also provide an ongoing conversation between the instructors and the teachers over the course of the semester.

TOOL 10. CELEBRATING LEARNING: CONNECTING TEACHERS, STUDENTS, AND FAMILIES

To begin each seminar portion of class, teachers share a celebration from their tutorials as well as a celebration "beyond" the course walls.

These celebrations normalize focusing on strengths. Regardless of how difficult a tutoring session might be, the tutors must consider and share a celebration with their classmates. Celebratory comments have included, for example:

> "My student was engaged for the entire hour. He wanted to read more!"

> "When he wrote the letter to his father, he really focused on audience."

> "She self-corrected tonight on her own for the first time. I was so excited."

> "I finally found a book that excited her."

Celebrations "beyond" the tutorial have included comments like:

> "I wrote letters to the families in my classroom asking them to tell me about their children and they all responded back."

> "Two of my students asked me to go to their church on Sunday. I learned so much about them from their families."

> "I've finally started asking critical questions in my classroom."

At the end of each semester, the teachers, students, and families gather together for a celebratory presentation: a space for students to share with their families and friends the culmination of a semester working together. For the students, who are often seen as those "who can't," this celebratory space is an opportunity to be recognized as capable. The students take on primary roles and speaking parts, which they are commonly denied in class or school events. Some become narrators. Others have the lead in the play, while still others choose security in masks as they perform. For the celebration, students select a reading from a favorite text, choose a piece of writing or a book they have written over the course of the semester, or, more recently, create PowerPoint presentations. In addition to an individual performance, each student also works with a partner or a group of three to develop another performance. In past semesters, these have included plays (with and without props), cooking events, interactive origami constructions, readers' theater, musical events, mystery whodunits, riddles, science experiments, and basketball demonstrations with accompanying written instructions. In a recent semester, Jawaan, a fifth-grade student, took the microphone after the performances and asked the parents and the children to "give a hand to our dedicated tutors who help us learn to read and write."

The celebration brings together mothers, fathers, brothers, sisters, cousins, aunts, uncles, grandmothers, grandfathers—all are invited and encouraged to attend. Parents whose children have been in the program over time comment on the students' growing competence as public speakers. As one mother noted while she watched the performance, "Look at her. In the beginning she wouldn't talk. Now look at her go." As each child performs, cameras flash and video cameras record the event. We learned the importance of the celebration from one family when the father asked Cheryl, on the first day of tutoring in September, when the final performance would be. This father, with three children attending the program, needed that much time to arrange time off from work so he could attend the celebration during the first week in December. Our past few semesters have generated 100% attendance by families at these events.

For the teachers, the celebration provides another opportunity to become comfortable with the students and their families. The enthusiastic turnout continues to break down stereotypes the teachers have held about parents not caring about their children's schoolwork. It also provides an authentic purpose for projects, an audience, and a deadline. After the performance, as the students, teachers, and families sit together, eat together, and learn from one another, the learning community broadens and strengthens.

TOOL 11. REFLECTIVE ESSAY: SYNTHESIZING LEARNING

The reflective essay is written at the end of the class, indeed, program, and encourages teachers to step back from the in-the-middle-of-it thinking and to integrate their experiences. Writing these papers requires teachers to draw on the range of data they have collected from tutoring, student documentation, journals, reading responses, and other sources. These reflections are quite individual in nature, and through the essays, the teachers reveal the teaching tools that have had the greatest impact on their learning, teaching, and thinking. When we, along with the teachers, share our reflective essays on the final night of class, another layer of insight and community-building is produced. The following four excerpts from the reflective essays are typical and speak to the ways the teachers take up the tools from the course.

Jackie's opening paragraph of her reflective essay highlights the impact of the course readings and the centrality of the course conversations to her development as a teacher:

> I feel I have grown as a teacher as a result of many aspects of this class. This class pulled all of my previous classes and understandings together. Thanks to Bomer I have brought the critical literacy piece into my teaching. Thanks to Marie Clay, Regie Routman, and Carol Lyons, Diane DeFord, and GaySu Pinell, I have reading strategies to inform my teaching. In addition, I took a great deal of knowledge and teaching strategies from the conversations with my colleagues. I was able to benefit from their tutoring sessions as well as my own. The space set aside for discussion around the table provided me with ideas to push my own teaching forward.

Like Jackie, Marissa's final paragraph of her reflective essay speaks to the significance of learning from her colleagues. Marissa extends the definition of collegiality to include the voices of her student's family:

> In my final thoughts and reflections about my experiences in this class, I want to talk about my classmates and professor that helped me so much. I have learned so much from our "talks around the table." I have learned that I am successful, and we can learn *so* much from each other. I will never doubt the power of people! We all have so much to offer each other, and I truly appreciate what I have learned from every professional in our class. I believe that the conversations I had with Tim, his grandmother, and in our class are the most powerful part of this learning experience!

For Sasha, the actual writing of the reflective essay caused her to integrate her learning for the course. As she notes in this excerpt from her essay, she experienced her most intense learning at the end of the semester. It took the full semester for Sasha to connect with her student and to the tenets of the course.

> The past 4 months have been a combination of struggle, frustrations, self-doubt, late nights, bleary eyes—but leaving it at that would be one-dimensional and misleading. There have also been the times of excitement, connecting with my student, breakthrough, determination, and revelation. I must admit that most of the revelations have happened just in the last couple of

weeks. It is amazing how one can talk, listen, practice, write, respond, read (read some more!), and take in information, but not
necessarily put it together until some time has passed and the
mind becomes open enough to make the connections. Or until
push comes to shove and one is staring reality right in the face!
This is what I feel has finally happened for me.

Many teachers find that the course itself is the tool for pulling
together the threads of their literacy specialist program. Linda, in her
final essay, uses the metaphor of a camera to comment on the impact of
the entire course experience in integrating her learning in the program.

Imagine looking through a camera lens, ready to take a photograph. You can see all of the components of the picture but many
parts are rather fuzzy. The camera is out of focus. With a slight
turn of the dial, the picture suddenly becomes clear and you can
see how all the parts fit together.
      Throughout 4 years of classes, I had in view the components
of effective literacy instruction. ERDG 620 (The Literacy Lab)
was the lens I needed to bring everything into focus for a clear
understanding of how they fit together.

Through hearing the essays, the sense of different learning paths
becomes evident. As teachers highlight their most significant moments
of learning in this intensive course experience, a need for the range of
tools offered during the course becomes evident.
      During the final night of class, teachers also acknowledge their
conflict of completion. While they have completed their master's degrees and their required formal course of studies, the teachers note
the lack of opportunities outside the course and program space for
collaborating with colleagues. Most say they believe their learning is
just beginning. The writing of the reflective essay in the context of the
learning community enables teachers to confront their learning histories and to consider their learning trajectories as professionals and
public intellectuals.
      The next two chapters by previous participants in the class docu-
ment the significant experiences in the class and their transfer to their
current practice. Once again, the impact of the tools is evident in both
chapters. In chapter 11, Jennifer Grand weaves her learning from the
Lab into her current practice, building book discussion groups with
families and building critical literacy. Chapter 12, written by Susan
Garnett, shows the power of journals and the connection to families,
and how this transferred into her teaching practice over several years.

11

Learning Is Continuous

JENNIFER GRAND STEIL

I was in my third year of teaching middle school (grades 6, 7, and 8) English Language Arts during my final class, before graduating with a master's degree in Reading. The pressure was on for the teachers in the Literacy Lab, not only because of the workload, but because we were responsible for working with, and helping, an actual reluctant reader.

THE LAB EXPERIENCE

I had the privilege of working with Ethan, who was in fifth grade. Ethan was an outgoing boy with a terrific sense of humor who loved sports and art. Ethan lacked self-esteem, noticing that other students were better at reading and writing than he was. The wonderful part of all the hard work in the lab was that we saw improvement in the reading and writing of each child we tutored. It took time, but it happened. I, along with my classmates, witnessed the effectiveness of all that I had struggled so hard to learn throughout my graduate education. This class changed the way I approach teaching.

I was actually a part of the Literacy Lab for three semesters. First I was a student, and then I continued my participation as a teaching assistant for the following two semesters. In this chapter, I reflect on the specific learning experience of the Literacy Lab and then illustrate how I have incorporated this learning into my work as a teacher and learner with middle school students.

Paying Close Attention

There are several things I learned in the Literacy Lab that I consider extremely valuable in my teaching of reading. First, I needed to pay attention to the needs and interests of my student, Ethan, during our tutoring sessions. I had to focus on the literacy understandings he already possessed and then move him forward from there (Lyons, 1993).

Using Specific Praises and Prompts

Second, I learned there is a real power to using positive reinforcement. I needed to use appropriate prompts while Ethan was reading, and reinforce the skills and strategies he already used (Fountas & Pinnell, 1996). I don't know how many people told me this before, but I never really "got it" until I learned how to use praise points with Ethan. Empty comments like "good job" or "nice work" don't hold any meaning to a child. However, when I praised Ethan for using a specific strategy, he would repeat the strategy in later readings. It was important to carefully select my language choices when prompting a student during reading or writing.

Ethan was actually with me for his second experience in the Literacy Lab. As Ethan read, he did not self-correct. He would miscue on a word, substituting a word that did not make any sense, and keep reading. When he was asked to self-correct (e.g., "Did that sound right?" or "Let's go back and take a look at that word again"), he would start to spell the word out backward. When asked why he was doing that, Ethan stated, "The teacher told me to start at the end of the word." I realized how important our prompts are for children—they are listening to what we tell them.

I now try to respond to my middle school students by telling them specifically what they are doing well. I make them aware of what skill or strategy they are already using well, and then show them a way to move forward. I start conversations with students about their reading or writing with something like "I like the way you worked on that lead," and then I try to share one or two strategies they might want to try. Students are then aware of the skills they already have, and have a strong base to develop self-extending systems as readers and writers.

Modeling Reading and Writing

Creating a safe environment for my students to feel comfortable as readers and writers is also extremely important. In order for students to truly learn and grow, they need to feel confident they can be successful (Cambourne, 1995). Modeling my own reading and writing during tutoring or class is one way I do this. I let students see my messy handwriting in my writer's notebook. I share my writing, with all the cross-outs and mess-ups still written on the page. I show them how my brainstorming for a writing piece does not always look like a nice web or an organized outline. I show them how I move things around in my writing, take parts out, or struggle with finding the right words. Often I write on an overhead in front of students, thinking out loud as I write. As a result, the students are not afraid to share their writing with me or their peers. They are also not afraid to struggle with their writing or ask for help.

Choice in Reading: Teachers and Students

During each tutorial session with Ethan, I gave him a choice of two to three books to read. I selected books based on his reading level and his interests. For example, toward the end of the semester, we decided to read a book titled *Skinny Bones* by Barbara Park (1997). I selected this book as an option for Ethan because it was at his instructional reading level and it was a humorous book about a boy on a baseball team, drawing on his interests.

After seeing how giving a choice in text affected Ethan's enthusiasm and willingness to work in the Literacy Lab, I began giving my students more opportunity for choice in what they were reading in my middle school classroom. Instead of selecting what books I think my students should read, I now give them the opportunity to choose. If we are studying a specific genre, for example, I pull as many books off the shelf as possible within that genre, and let the students select what book might be most interesting to them. Other times the students work in book groups, where they have two or three books to choose from within the content or style of writing we are studying. I found that students are more likely to actually read (and finish) the book if they are the ones who select it. Not only did Ethan enjoy reading *Skinny Bones* in our tutorial sessions, he continued to read the book at home.

Reading Levels

Before I send the students off to choose a book on their own, I teach them how to select a book that will be both interesting to them and on their reading level. Leveling books so I can assist students in their book choices is important (Fountas, 1996). When I was a student in the Literacy Lab, I learned the importance of finding an instructional reading level for fluency, problem-solving, and comprehension. If children select a book because it is what their friends are reading, the cover looks cool, or it is the shortest book available, they often find that the book is too difficult or too boring. So we discuss how to choose a book. I never really thought that a child would need to be shown how to do this, but I found that many struggling readers do not think there are books out there that they *can* read and enjoy.

I now give my students a lesson on how to select a "just right" book (Ohlhausen & Jepsen, 1992). A "just right" book is one that the student can read and comprehend with some challenge, but without assistance. I help them see how they normally choose books and demonstrate that there are going to be books that are too hard, too easy, and just right for all readers. Each reader is different. What is too hard for one person might be just right for another. We also talk about what happens when we read a book that is too hard or too easy. The students agree that they lose interest in books that are too hard, and often leave them unfinished. I place a variety of books of all different reading levels on their desk, and they sort them into piles of too hard, too easy, and just right. I rarely have the students all reading the same book. If we are going to read a text as a whole class, it will be one that we read and discuss together, out loud.

Guidance

I try to guide my students to appropriate and interesting books through my knowledge of the students as readers, and my knowledge of young adult and children's literature. I have seen a monumental change in the way my students feel about books since *I* started reading the young adult literature available in my classroom and the school library. This gives me a greater knowledge of books to suggest to students, and I also have the opportunity to level the books. This makes me better equipped to recommend books of interest and appropriate level to all students in my class (Fountas & Pinnell, 1996). I am constantly sharing with my students what I am reading, and my thoughts, predictions, and questions about each book as I read it. This is a way of modeling exactly what I am teaching them. I want my students to enjoy reading, and one way to do that is to share and discuss books! I expect my students to be reading the New York State–required 25 books a year, and therefore, I, too, read at least 25 books during the school year. If I do not continuously read the books that are available to young readers, how can I possibly suggest books to my students? How can I understand their frustrations about certain books or authors if I don't read them? How can I expect my students to enjoy reading if I don't enjoy reading?

Book Clubs—Talking About Books

As a result of this discovery, my Literacy Lab class decided to create a book group. We met every couple of weeks for close to a year to read and discuss children's literature and authors. I continued this tradition after my first semester of being a teaching assistant in the Literacy Lab, and that group of future reading teachers also met to discuss literature in a book group setting.

Sparking Interest

Both Ethan and Stuart (another student who was being tutored by a member of the Lab class) were reading books from the *Marvin Redpost* series (e.g., Sachar, 1993). The other tutor and I began our first meeting by asking the students about what the character Marvin was like in each of their books. Seeing that the character's personality was consistently portrayed prompted the boys to ask each other about similarities or differences in their books. Ethan asked Stuart if Marvin got in trouble in his book. He told Stuart that Marvin got into trouble with a substitute teacher in the book he was reading. Stuart responded, and then later asked Ethan if Marvin had a pet lizard in his book. The boys began talking without our assistance. Although they later read different books by different authors, they continued to meet to discuss literature. This helped Ethan discuss what he was reading more naturally, and encouraged him to read more books outside the tutorial setting so he could discuss them with Stuart.

Sharing Books and Strategies

When I start talking about a book I am reading with my middle school classes, at least five or six students in the class pick up the same book to read. They also enjoy it when I read and discuss the books they recommend to me. A special relationship develops between readers. Former students of mine still e-mail or contact me to tell me about a book they read that they think I would enjoy. We, as a class community, know each other as readers. We also get to know each other as individuals through literature. My students know what genres I love, and what genres I struggle through. They push me as a reader in the same way I try to challenge them as readers.

I have a regular reading workshop time, and special times set aside for book group meetings. After the first few weeks of working in a book group, where several students are reading the same book, my class virtually runs by itself. Before working in book groups I run several mini-lessons focusing on what good readers do when they read. We talk about reading strategies: visualizing the text, predicting, making connections, and asking questions as we read. In each mini-lesson I model the reading strategy, and then the students try it on their own. When we eventually start working in book groups, the students monitor their own reading strategies and those of their peers.

Taking Responsibility

The students have a lot of responsibility in their group. As a group they need to figure out the amount of reading they will need to do for each meeting. I give them the date the book is due, and they need to calculate how many pages they need to read each night, and for each individual book group meeting. Meetings are conducted every 2 to 3 days, on a preannounced schedule. The students also rotate jobs. One student is in charge of creating questions, another finds interesting vocabulary, another illustrates, one makes connections to life or other books, and another student makes predictions. Each student must be in charge of at least one job for the upcoming meeting. The jobs repeat the strategies that good readers use, giving the students more practice in using these strategies. Once the groups are up and running, I rotate around the room.

In addition to the assigned books for the class, the students are also expected to read a variety of books on their own. They have a reading folder where they keep track of the title, author, genre, and number of pages of each book they read. They also note the amount of time it took for them to read the book, and give each book a rating. I also give them the challenge of reading at least one book in every genre within the school year. They keep track of that as well, checking off each time they read a book on a list of the genres kept in their individual reading folders.

Keeping Track

I also keep a reading/writing folder for each student. In my folder I keep a collection of formal and informal assessments. I keep any running records taken, notes from mini-conferences during reading workshop, and reading and writing interest inventories from the beginning of the year and the end of the year. When I first started teaching middle school, I did not think there would be any use for taking running records. With 125 students, I didn't see how it would even be possible. However, since I learned so much about Ethan as a reader through analyzing running records of his reading, I began to reconsider. I realize that taking running records for all of my students would be impossible and unproductive, but analyzing running records for my struggling readers often provides me with important information for creating individualized reading instruction (Fountas & Pinnell, 1996).

During reading workshop my students get used to me stopping by and discussing what they are reading with them. It is during this time that I might ask a student to read a small section out loud so that I can take a running record. Through analyzing the running record, I can see whether or not the student is reading a book at his level. I can also see what strategies he uses to figure out words he is unsure of. Once I know what strategies he already knows and uses, I can begin moving him forward by expanding or adding new strategies. The running record analysis also is useful when meeting with parents about what strategies they should be working on at home.

TRANSFERRING LEARNING BEYOND THE LAB

The reading program I run in my class stemmed from a variety of places. It all began when I sat as a student in Literacy Lab. It was in the course that I realized there was so much more to teaching reading than assigning a book and giving questions to answer as the students read. There are many ways to assess student comprehension. I had read and gone to workshops about informal assessment, but never saw how it would be possible in a middle school classroom. I have 43 minutes with each class and 23 to 27 children in a class: a grand total of approximately 125 students. I could see how an elementary teacher could fit some of these assessments in, but where would I find the time? Well, that is still hard to answer. Each year I rethink and rework what goes on within my classroom. The students now know what is expected of them, and aside from mini-lessons and individual reading conferences, the students run reading workshop. The students are empowered by their responsibility in the process.

Teaching Writers, Not Writing: The Development of My Writing Program

During the Literacy Lab, I learned a lot about working one-on-one with a student in writing. Initially, Ethan resisted writing during our tutorial sessions. He would write one sentence, and then stop. When

I would ask him why he didn't like to write, he commented that his teacher told him his sentences didn't make sense. Throughout our time together, Ethan began to write complete stories and letters with detail, humor, and voice. His self-confidence grew, and he would ask to work on writing. While working on writing in tutorial sessions with Ethan, I became aware of the importance of giving students an authentic purpose for writing. There are a variety of ways to do this. Most importantly, I try not to give my students writing assignments for which there are no published models in the real world. Students need to see a purpose in what they are doing. For every writing assignment I try to present the students with some models of that particular style of writing; for example, if we are writing commentary articles, we look at examples of commentaries in magazines and newspapers.

Ethan especially loved Making Words activities (Cunningham, 1999; Pinnell & Fountas, 1998). Word study activities were effective in teaching Ethan spelling patterns. Ethan loved this activity each session and always looked at it as a game. He constantly wanted me to ask him to spell "hard" words. It made this type of learning enjoyable for him, and I found that he developed as a speller in ways he probably wouldn't have otherwise.

Just as with reading, my class discusses what good writers do. They keep a writer's notebook, collecting ideas and experimenting with various styles and techniques in writing. They go back to their writer's notebooks for ideas for formal pieces of writing. The students are given examples of authors who use a notebook to collect ideas. They are also given models of the styles and techniques of writing that they are experimenting with (Fletcher, 1996).

Constructing a Relationship with Families

While reading the book *Engaging Families* (Shockley et al., 1995) during my coursework in Literacy Lab, something hit me that I had not thought about before. I had never really considered the importance of getting parents involved in their child's education. Even though this book focuses on the elementary level, I still think it has merit at the middle school level. Making a connection with parents was something I thought would be impossible at the middle school level. It is so hard for parents to become a part of their child's education once they reach this stage of education; there is a feeling that parents are not welcome, both by the children and the teachers. Many middle school children resist help from their parents, and teachers often want the students to start taking more responsibility for their own education. And the parents feel their children are old enough to succeed on their own. The problem is, they still need guidance to be successful.

This belief in a child's independence can begin before middle school as well. Ethan's mother enrolled him in the Literacy Lab because she didn't know how to encourage him to read or write. He was struggling in school. She resisted coming in to observe our tutorial sessions at first, feeling that I was the expert. She didn't see how her involvement could matter. As the semester progressed, however, she began coming into the lab more and more. When she did attend, she became an active participant, reading along and discussing the text. Ethan looked up to his mother and even commented that she was the best reader he knew. Having her there and seeing that she enjoyed reading with him built his enthusiasm and excitement for reading.

Inviting Information

In my middle school classroom, I send home a newsletter at the beginning of the year to the parents of my students. This is something I had always done, but now I ask for something back: I invite my parents to write me a letter about their child. I have 125 students, and it is very hard to get to know them as individuals at the beginning of the year. Parents can write anything they want, and there is no set style or format. Over the past 3 years, I've received an average of 110 letters each year in response to 125 invitations. Most of the letters begin with comments like, "Thank you for wanting to get to know my child," or "Thank you for giving me the opportunity to write about my child." These letters allow me to get to know something personal about each child (and parent/family) right from the beginning of the school year. It also lets the parents know that I am interested in a partnership with them. Although I do not get a response from every parent, the many families who do respond make the activity worthwhile.

Starting a Parent–Teacher Book Group

Each year I try to increase my connection with parents. During my time in the Literacy Lab, I read an article about a parent–teacher reading group (Zaleski, 1999). In another attempt to connect, I started the Parent and Teacher Book Group. Once a month I meet with parents to read and discuss young adult literature. I begin the group each year by asking parents what they would like to see happen, or what they would like to gain from the group. The book group meetings develop from there. I have no formal way of running the meetings; they develop based upon the needs and interests of those in attendance. We sit around a conference table and share our thoughts about the books we read.

The books are selected in a variety of ways. We look at new literature, what the kids are reading, what books are causing controversy, how to broaden a child's reading selection, how to challenge our avid readers, and how to hook our reluctant readers. We discuss our opinions about the books, and whether our children would like the books. With controversial texts, we discuss whether or not we want our children reading them and why.

The group has developed over the past 3 years. Initially, I had a fluctuating group of seven parents. This year I have over 20! Parents do not need to make a full-year commitment and can attend any of the meetings. In my first year, I only invited the parents of my current students. Now former members continue as well. There are parents of sixth-, seventh-, and eighth-graders in the group. The increase in numbers has been one way to evaluate the interest of the parents. I have also tried to evaluate the book group through more formal means. Comments and discussions during the meetings have guided most of the changes that have developed in the program. At the end of the school year I ask participants to answer a written evaluation, asking what worked well for them and what changes they would like to see in the future. Some of the changes that have been made this year are: children will be invited to one to two meetings during the year, all members will create a written review of the books read, and book reviews will be summarized and made available for all middle school students and their families on the school Web site.

My assessment about the power of the book group is confirmed when I ask the parents what they have gained from the group. I have had a variety of responses to this question, but all are positive. Many parents comment that they now have a greater awareness of what books are available for their children. They also have a new appreciation for young adult literature. Parents have stated that their relationship with their children has changed; they now have something non-confrontational to talk about at the dinner table. Parent, teacher, and child are engaged in a continuous discussion about books. We share the books we are reading with each other, and recommend books to each other. My relationship with the families involved has also changed. Through our meetings, I gain a deeper understanding of my students by getting to know their families.

MY SELF-EXTENDING SYSTEM

Building a self-extending system was one of the central concepts in the Literacy Lab (Clay, 1993a). I have learned how to push myself forward in my own learning. I always considered myself a learner: someone open to new ideas and willing to experiment with new things in my classroom. In my beginning years of teaching, I followed the lead of the teachers around me and searched for creative ways to present lessons. I attended many conferences and workshops for teaching. I regularly read teaching magazines and spoke to my colleagues about what they were doing in their classrooms. I wanted to be an effective teacher. I wanted to make a difference in the lives of my students. However, I continued to feel frustrated with my own teaching. I felt as if there were gaps. I was teaching the students reading and writing, but I wasn't convinced they were growing as learners.

This final practicum course did not alter my willingness to change; it showed me where to begin. And once I got started, there was no stopping! The course gave me a worldview of teaching: the research, the theories, the resources, and the controversies. Not only did I learn about them, I was given a space to try out new ideas in a *safe* tutorial setting. As a result, who I am as a learner and as a teacher has grown.

Through the two semesters after I graduated that I spent as a teaching assistant in the Literacy Lab, I began to see why this course had such an affect on its members. Members of the course were seen as individual learners, moving forward from where they were in their experiences and knowledge of teaching. The class members were frequently told what they were doing well, and what they could do to move forward. The class took time to discuss all the reading and writing they were doing in and out of class. No comments were dismissed, and all ideas or thoughts were acceptable. Members shared what was working for them, and shared where they struggled. They also celebrated their successes.

I learned a lot about myself as an educator, and saw that I had valuable knowledge to share with others. I learned to guide other teachers toward trying new ideas without forcing my beliefs upon them. Through this experience I gained the confidence to mentor student teachers in my middle school classroom. I finally felt like I knew how to help them grow as teachers and learners.

As I look back over all the ways I have grown over the last few years, I continue to question my teaching and how I can continue to develop. That is the gift I was given by being a part of this class. I won't settle; I see how important it is to continue to read about the changes in education, the theories being discussed, and the people making these changes and having these discussions. I thrive on new knowledge and get excited about new ideas. That is what makes teaching so thrilling; each year there are new students to learn from and new lessons and theories to try and develop.

12

Following the Lead: Connecting with Families Through Journals

Susan Garnett

I had recently completed coursework for a bachelor's degree in special education when I entered the master's program in Reading at the University at Albany. As a student at the university, I completed a practicum at the Literacy Lab. It was during this time that I was matched to tutor Billy. Billy was a sixth-grade boy who was reading below grade level and whose parents were very involved in his academic work. Billy also had a sister in the Literacy Lab during that same semester. One of the requirements in the Literacy Lab was to establish a parent or home–school connection. This was the first time I had encountered the idea of using home journals to communicate with parents.

CONNECTING WITH FAMILIES—A STARTING POINT

Cheryl, our Lab instructor, first introduced the family journals (see chapter 4) as part of our readings from *Engaging Families* (Shockley et al., 1995). Initially, I confess, I saw the family journals as an assignment to be completed. They were required on the syllabus, and I needed to fit them into my very busy calendar. However, reading this book was important for me. As a parent, I wanted my own children's teachers to respect the literacy values we shared in our home. Since I love to share stories about my own children, I thought other parents would like to share theirs as well. Additionally, children like to read what others have written to them and about them. I can remember going through a strongbox my mother saved. The inside of this box contained pieces of writing we had written and cards and letters from relatives. I loved going through the box and rereading old cards and letters. I began to see the journals as a way to continue the conversations Billy's mom, Melanie, and I shared after each tutoring session. One afternoon in February, I asked Melanie to come in a bit early to discuss the journals. I mentioned during our conversation that the journals would be a way for us to discuss Billy's progress throughout the program. However, I had little idea how powerful the journals would become during my conversations with Melanie over the course of the semester.

Early in the semester, I didn't know very much about Billy or his family's expectations for his involvement with the Literacy Lab. I came to learn that his family wanted Billy "to get through the school day with as little discomfort as possible." We were all concerned about Billy accelerating as a reader.

For the first journal entry, I asked Melanie to begin by writing what she loved about Billy. Enclosed within the journal was a letter I wrote to Billy's parents:

Dear Melanie & John,
I am delighted we will be working together. This journal will provide an opportunity for all of us to discuss and collaborate on some of the things Billy and I will be accomplishing. The program I have outlined places a positive emphasis on what Billy knows, then proceeds to build on those foundations. Sometimes I will ask you to share stories in this journal for Billy to read. Childhood experiences are sometimes a good way to begin. They can include experiences like being on a sports team, fishing, favorite relatives, what you enjoyed doing as a child, friendships, family traditions, etc. These stories will provide another source of reading for Billy, as well as encourage his ongoing efforts. Billy will also be sharing some of his experiences with you in his journal writing.
A little bit about myself—I have a degree in special education. I am currently in the Masters program at the University at Albany where I will attain a reading degree. On a personal note, I have three children, all boys. Their ages are seven, fourteen, and sixteen (my oldest just started driving). As you know, parenting is a full time job, and well worth it! I love children and teaching. I cannot think of anything I would enjoy doing more

. . . well, maybe living in the Bahamas, under the sun, enjoying a cool breeze from the ocean. Dreaming is fun!

I look forward to our conversations as we move through the program together. :0)

Sincerely,
Susan

Each evening when we convened around the table as part of the class, we talked about the family connections that had been made that evening. We discussed what we were learning about our students and what was going well. I was pleased with the responses from Melanie and was quite surprised to discover that my colleagues in class had not received responses from their families. It never occurred to me that Melanie might not respond. Indeed, another teacher in our group, who was tutoring Billy's sister, had not received any responses in the home journal from Melanie, while I had already received several responses from Melanie, as well as Billy's other family members. What I learned through the community of inquiry in the around-the-table conversations with my colleagues and professor (Wells, 2001) was that the success of the journal begins with the "language" of the journal. I realized this as we discussed why the same parents were responding differently to the home journals. My colleagues asked me how I had written the journals. I explained that I approached the journals through the lens of a parent. When I wrote the introductory invitation to Melanie, I wrote it as one parent to another. Through this journal, we all learned together, and followed each other's lead (Clay, 1993b). We all became a community of learners collaborating together toward a shared interest—the success of Billy.

One of the ways I used the journal to guide instruction was to look for opportunities for instructional spaces within the journal entries. In one entry, Melanie shared how Billy was devoted to playing the trumpet. She shared that he woke up early 2 days a week to attend before-school band rehearsal. Melanie wrote in the journal that she loved to sit and listen to Billy play, "because each time he plays he gets better and better." When I learned about Billy's interest in the trumpet, I brought in recordings I had of Louis Armstrong. Our connection to Armstrong's music turned into something quite unexpected.

As Billy was reading *Maniac Magee* (Spinelli, 1993), I was guiding him to focus on imagery. I asked him to listen to Armstrong's recordings and the lyrics to gain an awareness of powerful description. Shortly after that, an article appeared in the *New York Times* about Armstrong. This was another tie-in for us, since the chapters we were reading in *Maniac Magee* focused on segregation. As Billy read through the newspaper article on Armstrong, he noticed that it also talked about segregation. Afterward, Billy brought the article home to share with his dad. The next time Billy met with me, he said, "I didn't know it, but Louis Armstrong is my dad's favorite musician!"

EXTENDING THE JOURNALS FROM THE LITERACY LAB TO THE CLASSROOM

One criticism of the journals is that they are too difficult to maintain with many children. In the following sections, I discuss extending the journals from a one-on-one tutoring arrangement to my work as a reading specialist. After I graduated from the Literacy Lab, I began family journals with students in a third-grade inclusion classroom. In my position, I was responsible for teaching six students with Individualized Educational Plans in their primary classroom. As a new teacher, I did not want to take on too many responsibilities at one time. I thought working with my six students would be a nice way to begin; I would have the chance to develop a relationship with their families. During the first few days of the school year, I organized the journals and included my original letter from the Literacy Lab. I sent the journals home on Tuesday and asked for parents to return them to school on Thursday. The parents liked the idea and responded each week. All six families included wonderful responses in the journals. In most cases, *both* parents wanted to share something about their child.

> Josh is my boy who is nine years old. He is my pride and joy. He is growing into a young man with a heart of gold. Some days he makes mom feel real old. He likes to play sports and likes to build forts. He likes to ride his dirt bike, and occasionally take a hike. He enjoys swimming most of all and then it's basketball and football . . . . His favorite food is his dad's chili. He likes it spicy hot isn't that silly . . . . Josh is a very sensitive, caring, compassionate young man. I think he is the Best! Thank you God for landing him in my nest!
>
> > All my love forever,
> > Mom

Josh's dad wrote:

> Josh is a great son. We go to our camp and go fishing. He also likes to ride his motorcycle. Josh loves to talk about 4-wheelers

and go-carts, and motorcycles. At night, we like to watch Celtic
games. In the afternoon Josh practices football playing both of-
fense lineman & defense tackle. His physical makeup suits him
well in football. Josh is a very sensitive and caring little boy. I
would like him to go to college.

Dad

The comments that the parents wrote in the journal provided me
with a window to understanding each child's family. I encouraged
parents to share family traditions, favorite books, and special holidays.
I encouraged the parents to pass the journals along to other family
members: grandparents, uncles, aunts, cousins, and siblings. I used
the journals to guide my instruction for book selections, writing pieces,
and open conversations. The students wanted to read about their family histories. The journals encouraged the students to read. The readings were meaningful to the students, and writing in the journal was
meaningful for the parents as well. In the first entry, I always asked
the parents to tell me something wonderful about their child and what
they love about them. I wanted the journals to be a place of celebration, a discourse between teachers and families.

Because I opened the journal with, "Tell me about your child," the
journal was an ever-evolving dialogue with parents from the start.
This conversation was always between learners and teachers. I, as the
"formal" teacher, did not have all of the answers. Rather, the family
became my teacher.

About a month or so after the start of school we had Open House:
"Meet the Teacher Night." During this gathering, parents come to
school to discuss the curriculum with teachers. I explained the Language Arts curriculum and the purpose of the family journals. The
other teacher in the room explained the math and science curriculum.
When we opened the floor for questions, many of the parents who had
not been invited to participate in the journals (since their children
were not "technically" my students) inquired into what they called the
"Memory Journal." They shared that they had heard about the journals
and were feeling left out of the process. Following their lead, I then
opened the journals to anyone who wanted to participate. When I
agreed to do this, I confessed that I had never actually responded to
so many journals at one time. I also promised that I would do my best
to respond in a caring and thoughtful way to all of them. I wanted the
journals to remain personal and was worried about communicating
substantively with so many families. However, to my surprise, keeping up with the journals was not as difficult as I thought they might

be. I was driven by the excitement that others were as passionate about the journals as I was. I no longer wrote in the journals to discuss student achievement, as I had done with Billy and his family. Instead, I responded solely to their writing and insights about their children, and shared in their celebrations.

Week after week the journals rolled in and I responded to every journal, commenting and thanking each parent for their responses and insights to their children. Each time a parent wrote something, I used it to continue the conversation. I asked the parents to talk about their children's favorite baby moments, their favorite holidays, family traditions, favorite books, and first writing experiences. One parent even sent in an original piece she had written in third grade.

Parents shared favorite books that were read to them by their parents. In turn, I found these books in libraries and brought them in so their children could read and explore and marvel at how blessed they were to have the opportunity to read the very same book their parents read or had read to them. The students were excited and took the books home and shared them with their parents! These experiences expanded how I understood family literacy. Following the parent's lead, I changed the name of the journals from "family" to "memory" journals.

THE SECOND YEAR—JOURNALS ACROSS GRADE LEVELS

In the second year I became the only full-time reading specialist in the building, working with small groups of children in a pull-out program. Remembering how deeply the parents were involved in the journals the year before, I decided to use the journals across all of the grade levels (third, fourth, and fifth). Not only was I extending the journals beyond one classroom, my student assignment now increased to 34 students. When you are in a classroom, everyone becomes a family. When you provide a service, you become an extension of the family. As a reading specialist working in a pull-out situation, even though you may see the student every day, there is a component missing. The pull-out component changes the dynamics with students, classroom teachers, and parents. Now more than ever, the journals took on even greater importance. Building a connectedness with the children and their families through the journal was an essential key to my success with the students. In pull-out settings, reading specialists often do not communicate with the families because this is often seen as the primary responsibility of the classroom teacher. However, I knew that making rich connections with families could accelerate the literacy development of struggling readers. I once again looked for opportunities in the entries, and then incorporated these into lessons for the students.

When asked to "Share your favorite book at your child's age," one of the parents, Rachel, wrote that her favorite book was *Caps for Sale*. Rachel also shared favorite books for *everyone* in the family! The next day, when Molly saw *Caps for Sale* in my room, she had an immediate connection with the book. She took *Caps for Sale* home with her that evening to share with her mom. I found the entire list of favorite family books and provided them for Molly as well.

I think the journals not only deepened my connection with families and students, but also strengthened our connection as a community of learners. I honored their words by bringing what they had written into our daily lessons.

THE THIRD YEAR—COMPLICATING THE CONVERSATION

During my third year in the building, I made changes in my approach to the journals based on changes that occurred within my school and within the school district. In my third year in the district, another full-time reading teacher was hired. I shared the journals with her, as I had had positive feedback from the parents and success with students for the past 2 years. She liked the idea and wanted to institute the journals into her reading program. We discussed the importance of the opening invitation to parents and the impact of our language choices. However, despite our interest, the changes to our district were dramatic. A new districtwide instructional supervisor and a new Language Arts Coordinator for our building were hired. My student caseload increased to 50 students, and the state standardized test now consumed a large amount of instructional time.

For the first time, I understood the complexities for those who feel the constraints of teaching and managing the journals in a rigid environment. What was the difference between this year and the first year, when the parents were demanding to participate in the journal process? During my third year in the district, I was no longer given autonomy. The district's mandated program now focused on test preparation. The new policy did not fit with my philosophy of teaching. Making the journals work in previous years was positive. I found a way to make them productive, and they were successful for the students. Whether I had one or 20 journals going at one time, I saw first-hand the success they achieved with students, families, and teachers. However, in the last year, I could not find a way to navigate the journals within the structure of the newly mandated reading program. In view of the success I had had with the journals in previous years, I decided that I would institute them again in another district—one within a literacy philosophy that valued collaboration and developing partnerships with families.

CONTINUING THE CONVERSATION

For me, the journals were quite magical in the way they contributed to the success of my students. The journals had an intimacy that did not take place during brief "Meet the Teacher" nights and through occasional conversations with families. These conversations were sustained and were more personal, as they contained anecdotes, memories, and information that did not apply to any other student or any other family. The discussions and sharing focused exclusively on the most important person: the child. I think one of the most powerful indicators for me in knowing the journals were successful, besides seeing the students become better readers, was when parents came to me with their arms extended for hugs and kisses. When children see their parents hug their teacher, they know something is real about their connection. We all became partners in learning.

13

Developing Reflective Teaching

In this chapter we focus our attention on the teaching tools for examining and refining teaching practice and developing reflective teachers. Our intention with reflective practice is not simply to generate the passive reflection of observing oneself closely in a mirror, but to engage teachers in actively seeking patterns in their own practice and its consequences *as part of changing what they do.*

Initially, attending to complex instructional decisions and documenting them and their basis in the child's behaviors while teaching is very difficult, and we accept modest attempts. As the planning, noticing, and pedagogical decision-making become more automatic, dividing attention between the involvement of teaching and the documenting of teaching and learning becomes increasingly natural. Greater understanding of the patterns to be noticed also produces greater memory for those patterns.

The tools described in this chapter invite teachers to examine both themselves as observers, and the learning they do in the process of studying their own practice. They do this in the context of interactions with colleagues and students and their families, all of whom provide different reflections to complicate their understanding of their practice and of themselves as teachers. In particular, the teachers are required to examine their language and its implications for teaching and learning.

TOOL 12. DOCUMENTING TEACHING:
LEARNING TO NOTICE AND NAME

Although documenting what the child knows and how the child acts upon this knowledge is central to effective teaching, documenting the context in which the child knows and acts is equally important. Teachers are required to plan their teaching sessions, and also to document their in-process teaching-learning observations.

The Reading Instructional Log

The reading instructional log/planning sheet currently used for this documentation is shown in Figure 13.1. The practice was appropriated from Marie Clay (1993b) and transformed for our purposes. The reading and writing instructional logs feature the overlapping instructional components required during the hourlong tutorial: reading, writing, and word study. This tool works to make the activity of teaching conscious. The teachers are expected to complete the sections of the instructional logs marked with an asterisk prior to the tutorial.

The purpose and intent of the categories included in the reading instructional log/planning sheet are explained below.

Texts Used. Teachers indicate the texts they plan to use for each session, as well as the purpose for each text selection. Teachers specify the guided reading level and genre of the text, and note whether the text is a new text or a reread. This information is later transferred to a reading and writing log where teachers and students examine the range of genre and levels of texts read over the course of the semester. Teachers also include the number of words read during each session as one way to consider the child's stamina as a reader and the pace of instruction.

Book Introduction. Initially, book introductions are often difficult. Their function is to bring a book exactly into the child's zone of proximal development. It is not enough to arrange for the child to read the book. The introduction must arrange a context in which a child will encounter problems while being sufficiently engaged and knowledgeable to solve the problems. Without this, it is not possible to develop agency. For the teacher, this means knowing both text and child in sufficient detail to understand what it will take to build a bridge between the two. It means deciding which words and concepts to teach or foreground, and how, before the child reads. It also requires planning instruction for independence. On top of this, introductions must become conversational (for an example, see Nikki and Tekwan in Chapter 15).

Initially many teachers feel that they can improvise, and resist the need to thoroughly preplan. However, the process of writing insists that teachers confront these details and imagine the child's logic. Though they initially resist writing planned book (or chapter) intro-

FIGURE 13.1. Reading Instructional Log/Planning Sheet

Name_____   **Session #**____

Texts *	Book Introduction *	Strategic Reading	Word Study *	Critical Literacy *
Reread * Purpose Level Genre Choice: Student or Tutor?	Include: (1) Topics/content for instructional conversations (2) Words to preview *in context*	(1) Strategies used by the student (2) Strategies prompted by the tutor (INDICATE M, S, V) Use specific examples from text. Include student responses.	Mini-lessons	
Running Record * Purpose Level Genre Choice: Student or Tutor?				
New Read * Purpose Level Genre Choice: Student or Tutor?	*Discussion Prompts *** (Think conversation versus interrogation)			

* To be completed prior to session.

Key: M = meaning; S = syntax; V = visual.

122

ductions, they often subsequently remark on their effectiveness. Since teachers often use several texts during each session, many write their introductions on post-its for additional texts.

Discussion Prompts. As the teachers write possible prompts, they initially notice that it feels formulaic or stilted to do this before reading with the child. However, by requiring teachers to prepare prompts ahead of time, we can support them as they extend their interactions. As many of the teachers analyze their interactions during the audio or video analysis, this section of the log becomes more developed. They are often directed to the appendix of *"You Gotta Be the Book"* by Jeff Wilhelm (1997) to extend their questions when they are experiencing difficulty. Discussion prompts have included, "How would you feel if you were Marvin?" "Tell me about your favorite part of the book," "What have you learned about snakes?" "If you could learn more about snakes, what would you want to know?"

Strategic Reading. The strategic reading section is completed during the tutorial as the teachers engage with the students and observe their reading strategies and behaviors. The teacher indicates the strategies used by the student independently or prompted. Specific examples from the texts are required. During the semester, the teachers become more detailed and specific in their prompts to help the students become strategic, and are required to indicate if their prompts focus on meaning (M), syntax (S), or visual (V) cueing systems. For example, Amy notes her first-grade student's independence while reading a book on snakes. Her notes on his strategic reading include:

Page 15—when he read the word *down* he looked at the first letter "d," and then used the picture cues. (M)(V). He read *hole* for *home* and then self-corrected. (M)(S)(V).

At a glance, the teachers and instructors can examine which cueing systems are privileged by the teacher and by the student. This helps the teachers become more strategic in their prompting.

Word Study. In this section, teachers include the mini-lessons for word study during the lessons. The teachers and instructors look for patterns and the attending logic for the word study selections. Questions the instructors frequently ask when examining this section include: "How did you select this mini-lesson? What evidence do you

have to suggest that these are appropriate choices?" The teachers articulate their instructional decision-making as they respond to these
questions.

Critical Literacy. This section is initially one of the more difficult
spaces for the teachers, and becomes more detailed and specific over
the course of the semester. As the teachers engage in course readings,
they become more confident with exploring critical literacy within the
tutorial. Initial questions asked by the teachers focus on the author's
intent, such as "Why do you think the author wrote this book?" "What
do you think the author wanted the readers to learn from reading this
text?" Once the teachers become more confident, they are willing to
grapple with more difficult topics relating to race, gender, and the environment.

The Writing Instructional Log

The writing instructional log (Figure 13.2) is similar in design to the
reading log and includes the categories discussed in the following
paragraphs. Teachers are expected to complete several sections of this
log prior to the tutorial as well.

Topics/Genres. In this section, the teachers include the function
and audience for the pieces of writing generated during each session.
Guiding questions used to support the students as they engage in
writing are also expected. Initially, teachers focus on personal narratives to learn more about the students. For some of the students this
is difficult, since they are used to more formulaic writing in their classrooms. As the semester progresses, the teachers are expected to include
a range of genres in the tutorial, and articulate the function and audience for each. In the past, teachers have included letter writing, fiction,
nonfiction, poetry, plays, and PowerPoint presentations.

Strengths. As the teachers work with the students, they are required to first focus on the strengths of the writer. This is often a shift
for many of the teachers, as they initially attend to misspelled words
or incorrect grammar. Focusing on the strengths of the piece of writing
through content, voice, and language choices helps the teachers think
about the student's strengths and understandings as a writer.

Teaching Focus. In this section, the teachers focus on areas to address and mini-lessons that would support the learner. As with the

FIGURE 13.2. Writing Instructional Log/Planning Sheet

Name _____ **Session #** ____

Date _____

Genre * Topic * Include * (1) Purpose/Audience (2) Guiding Prompts	Strengths (1) Content (2) Voice (3) Language Choices (4) Conventions	Revision (content)	Word Study *	Critical Literacy *
	Focus * (1) Areas to Address (2) Mini-lessons	Editing (conventions)		

* To be completed prior to session.

reading section, instructors question how the mini-lessons were selected and what evidence was used to determine appropriate instruction. For example, we expect to see mini-lessons on writing leads and endings, text layout and organization, topic selection, using resources to find information, dialogue, making word choices, audience, voice, and many others. Teachers have extensive resources in their readings and class discussions to draw from.

Revision (Content)/Editing (Conventions). In this section, the teachers specify examples of revision and editing during the session. Teachers indicate whether revision and editing were initiated by the student or directed by the teacher. Revision and editing are not emphasized early in the semester. Our initial emphasis is on building students' authority—the sense that they have something to say and the confidence to say it. Once students have sufficient volume and fluency, and have found a piece they are committed to, revising and editing become more meaningful. Commitment to a piece also gives them the energy they will need to sustain the work of revising and editing.

Word Study. To plan for word study the teachers examine the students' writing to analyze the spelling and to look for conceptual patterns of misspelled words using *Words Their Way* (Bear et al., 2003) as a reference text. The teachers include specific examples from the text. For example, Kendra noted that Asia consistently wrote *becez* for *because.* Amy wrote

> [the focus will be on] *still* and *will.* When trying to spell *still* he chunked out the blend and said "it's the little word ill." When he came to *will* he said, "they rhyme so they might be spelled the same." We then used magnetic letters and spelled *pill, sill, mill, spill.*

Critical Literacy. As with reading, the critical literacy writing section often remains blank initially. As the teachers read the assigned articles and engage in community conversations, they add comments and details to this section. Examples include writing for a purpose, particularly to change injustices, and consideration of how to present an argument and in which medium.

Planning and Preparation. We see change in the documentation over the course of the semester. First, columns that were empty are attended to. Second, the documentation changes in its specificity. For example, we begin to see comments like, "Transferred word work to writing. Wrote *car* then stopped and said I need to add an *e* to make it *care*." The value in this documentation is that it allows both the teacher and instructor, by scanning several of the lesson logs, to notice patterns such as imbalances in instructional focus. Teachers must *plan* well to reduce the likelihood of problematic interactions and increase the likelihood of learning. They must also *prepare* well to deal with the unexpected results that following the student's lead can bring with it. In addition, they must be prepared to relinquish their plan or those aspects that prove less than optimal.

For example, one evening Sarah, arriving to teach 6th-grader Billy, and having planned carefully as usual, learned that his grandfather had just died. Her response was, "I have my plans. What do I do?" Cheryl suggested that she follow Billy's lead, and find out how he wanted to proceed. Sarah did, offering him some possibilities, and he elected to write about his grandfather. The entire teaching session was taken up by his writing a poem, which was later sent to his family and read at the funeral. This was the most extensive writing Billy had done, and he cried as he read the completed version. Billy's poem, in first draft form with temporary spelling, is included.

> Billy's Poem in First Draft Form
> I feel so sad.
> I did not think
> It would happen.
> He was the best.
> He gave me every
> thing even [when] it was
> not my birthday.
> It was weird.
> he went into the
> hositbul for a week.
> then he came
> out. I thought
> out was out for
> good. Then he went
> in. then he die. Now
> on Monday I'm going
> to see him. But he
> won't be looking at
> me. But I will always
> have him in my hart.

And I know he will
have me in his
hart. And no one
will replase him
in my hart. I feel
like I am part of
his body. His berd rubbed
up agaenst my face.
I miss his voice.
I miss him the most.
I hate to see my
grandmother in pane.
He would take me
out to eat.
when I
look at my mom
she is very sad.
My older sis
really
miss him. he
took her out for
ice cream after
school.
In school I wacthed
a movie. I was crying
because people were
dieing.

There is a delicate balance between planning and involvement that has been presented as a hallmark of quality teaching by Carol Lyons and her colleagues (Lyons et al., 1993). The zone of proximal development provides the relational and motivational infrastructure that enables students to extend themselves into areas of insecurity (Litowitz, 1993).

Anecdotal Record Sheet

Teachers are expected to include "quotable quotes" from the student, moments of puzzle, moments of celebration, and other noticings from the tutoring session. Like the other sections, examples are often sparse initially. As the semester progresses, teachers become more attentive to the child, and a broader range of behaviors and observations becomes meaningful and hence memorable.

TOOL 13. REFLECTIVE JOURNALS:
WRITING TO UNDERSTAND TEACHING

A second aspect of documenting teaching comes through reflective journals, which are completed immediately after each tutoring session. These structured journals provide the teachers with time and a routine to consciously take stock of their practice and to internalize the guided conversations that normally follow observations. The immediacy of this structured reflection enables the teachers to organize their teaching experience to inform future instruction, and to anticipate and productively address emotional threats to their instruction. The journals provide the space and the less tangible emotional data that enable theorizing about the difficult aspects of instructional interactions. These records are very much concerned with the business of becoming a teacher.

The logic of the daily reflective journal prompts reflects the logic of the debriefing sessions following an observation. The following is our list of prompts with explanations:

- *Student Learning (surprises and breakthroughs).* Student learning is a central focus, but surprises are particularly important indicators of false assumptions. We want teachers to automatically attend to feelings of surprise rather than suppressing them.
- *What went well, how I know, and why it went well.* As with any learner, we want teachers to attend first to what is going well, but also to check for evidence to be sure it is not just assumed to be going well. Theorizing about why it went well is central to building agency and extending control of practice.
- *What I will do differently next time, why I will do it differently.* Rather than lamenting error, teachers contemplate why something did not go as well as planned, and on the basis of that theorizing consider how, what, and why to change. In particular, are there necessary changes to short- and long-term goals?
- *Critical Literacy.* Teachers contemplate how they addressed issues of critical literacy in the session.
- *Uncertainties and Questions.* These should always be present and acknowledged. They can then be brought to the learning community for discussion, thus building the basis for (and expectation of) productive learning communities.
- *Connections to Readings.* Insisting on connections among readings and practice builds the habit of professional reading and con-

necting practice to that reading. This also builds the teacher's confidence as a public intellectual.

As with other aspects of the course, completing the journals is initially difficult, and we accept modest efforts and prompt for detail. Teachers often comment that they are unsure why their teaching has been productive or how to connect their teaching to the course (and program) readings. As expertise develops, teachers see the value in the journal. In her reflective essay, Mary commented on her experiences writing the journal over the course of the semester:

> When we first began tutoring I looked at the reflective teaching journal and all the different sections overwhelmed me. I thought to myself, how I am going to reflect on my sessions twice a week and fill out the journal? It was hard for me at first, but it did get easier as time went on. What worked well for me was reflecting on what went well during my session first and then reflecting on what I would do differently next time. It helped that the section was titled *What I will do differently next time*—not *What didn't work well?* Each time I came to this section I always reflected on what *I* needed to change to improve my tutoring session, but I never reflected on anything Jalinda did wrong or that I wanted her to do differently. It was always about how I could move her forward as a learner and help her to move towards independence.
>
> Spending time writing in our journals and then celebrating something from our tutoring session [in the community conversation] helped me to focus on the positive.

For our purposes, the journals are a structured way to sustain and internalize the dialogue of the personal observations when we are observing other teachers. They also provide a concrete focus of discussion for development and problem-solving. Earlier we used an open format for these reflections but found it a lot more difficult and time-consuming to shape productive reflection. The current format has lasted for 3 years with modest modification and has proven productive for both instructors and teachers. Karen Amundsen (see chapter 6) speaks about the leadership role she took in her building by advocating for debriefing/reflecting time in her schedule as a literacy specialist.

TOOL 14. OBSERVATION CONFERENCES: EXTENDING PRACTICE

As in any classroom, individual conferences serve an important function that cannot always be served in whole-class discussions. In our class, the instructor observes each teacher working with a student once a week, transcribes the tutoring session (using carbon paper to produce a second copy), and provides a nonjudgmental constructive conference—not unlike a writing conference. The predictable structure of the conference, like the reflective journal, includes "What went well?" "How can you tell?" "What would you like to change?" Just as we ask the teachers to follow the student's lead during the tutorial, in this space it is the instructor's job to follow the teacher's lead.

Just as in a writing conference or a response to reading, it is necessary to selectively attend to the most productive places for change: only one or two. Initially, teachers struggle with the details of book introductions, conversations about the text, responses to errors, and time spent reading and writing. Like the students, the teachers would be overwhelmed by having to attend to all of these features at once. This individual focus makes it possible to nudge teachers toward productive reflection in pivotal areas that others in the group might not need. This one-to-one interaction is a space in which difficult issues can be addressed that might not as easily be addressed in the group setting. For example, Joan notes in her final essay:

> Upon each of our observation sessions with either Cheryl or
> Ilene we would discuss what had been seen. During one of
> these talks Ilene opened my eyes to the question, "What's your
> purpose? What's your goal?" Although this had been talked
> about in class and mentioned in Cambourne (2002) it did not hit
> home until that moment. I had purpose in discussing parts of the
> word [during writing] with Nakresha, but they were not meet-
> ing my goal of her producing meaningful text. From that mo-
> ment on, I rethought what I wanted Nakresha to be accomplish-
> ing and focused more on her agenda rather than mine.

There are occasions when students are absent. On these occasions the teacher is required to observe other teachers and provide feedback in the manner modeled by the instructors—also using carbon paper. This gives the teachers a metacognitive understanding of the process and helps them make better use of their own conferences. This also gives the teachers the opportunity to see different cases and to co-theo-rize with their colleagues about what they are noticing.

TOOL 15. VIDEOTAPED LESSONS: CONFERRING WITH COLLEAGUES

For 20 years we used one-way viewing windows to collectively ana-lyze teaching in progress. These behind-the-glass conversations re-quired the teachers to notice teaching and learning interactions, talk about them in productive ways, and connect what they saw with what they had read. The conversations behind the glass produced external-ized thinking, and enabled the shaping of that thinking through the shaping of the conversations.

Teachers learn in these conversations how to represent students and other teachers constructively, and how to provide helpful feed-back to one another. They also are offered the instructional interactions of another as a metaphor through which to examine their own teach-ing. Teaching behind the glass requires getting over defensiveness about one's practice and learning to actively use the situation to ex-pand learning—and to open the possibility of subsequently modeling teaching practice for other teachers. Teachers also receive written feed-back from each of their peers, feedback that is sought and cherished.

With our move to the school site, we replaced the behind-the-glass conversations with conversations around videotaped tutoring sessions. The conversations remain much the same, except that the ob-served teacher is present for the conversation and manages, and frames, the presentation. There are, however, additional changes. Currently, teachers videotape their entire session once, selecting a 15-minute seg-ment to present to the group for feedback. The segment should be an area on which they are working and on which they would find feed-back helpful. We believe the process of selecting a "working" aspect of one's practice to examine with others leads to useful long-term prac-tices and attitudes. Making the selection requires an immediate analy-sis and reconnection with feelings and experiences during the tutoring session. It also requires consciously choosing to present oneself as vul-nerable, anticipating feedback with trust. Using the videotaped ses-sion also allows us to freeze the pedagogical action to talk about what we notice and offer different instructional possibilities. With written feedback from each colleague in hand, and the experience of the dis-cussion, the teacher can, with some distance, analyze the range of op-tions and interpretations offered by the members of the class.

The following transcript provides an example from Angela's presentation of her video of writing time in which she is using K-W-L (What I Know, What I Want To Know, and What I Learned) (Ogle, 1986) and reading a book on sea turtles to generate nonfiction writing with her fifth-grade student. The videotape runs continually. As the tape runs, Cheryl asks questions of the group as they watch, so the spacing among the interactions below is uneven, but connected to the video action:

Cheryl: Talk about what just occurred.

Shelly: She's introducing a strategy.

Cheryl: Think about the modeling so far.

Nancy: She's making the purpose clear and setting him up for the writing.

Wendy: He's focused.

Angela: He talks when he writes.

Cheryl: What's interesting in what he's doing?

Shelly: He's thinking.

Cheryl: You want to model asking a question for the W part of the [KWL] chart.

Cheryl: What just happened?

Donna: It's a hook for his reading [to help him answer questions for the W on the K-W-L].

Wendy: She is using lots of opportunities to have him read.

Cheryl: What else are you noticing?

Laurie: I like the drama, acting it out a little bit. It helps you visualize.

Cheryl: What are you noticing?

Christine: When they are working together, they are bent toward each other.

Wendy: Angela is modeling a level of enthusiasm.

Cheryl: What is he doing right here?

Laurie: Revising.

Angela: I'm not sure he has done that before.

It is still early in the semester, and Cheryl is prompting principally for what the teachers are noticing about what is going on and talking about practice. Angela, whose tape it is, is one of the discussants, and she notices at the end something she hadn't noticed while teaching. Though not all of the teachers are involved in commenting during this brief segment, all must comment in the process of the session (a record is kept of contributions, and teachers are prompted when

necessary). Although not commenting does not indicate lack of participation in the conversation, we keep track of who is actively participating and encourage teachers who are reticent.

In a second example, midway through the semester, Amy is working with Tekwan, a second-grader, revising a piece of his writing. As
the video runs, Cheryl prompts:

> *Cheryl:* Talk about that. What did you notice?
> *Christine:* He was monitoring his reading through his writing.
> *Cheryl:* Talk about the interaction.
> *Wendy:* She showed him where he repeated and asked him what
> he wanted to do. He had control.
> *Cheryl:* What's the purpose of this part?
> *Jillian:* Revising.
> *Amy:* For meaning, it didn't make sense.
> *Cheryl:* You said, "What did you want it to say?" Why is this a
> helpful prompt?
> *Kelly:* He's saying, "Oh, that's what I want to write." Right now
> he's focusing on what I have to fix instead of what I want to
> say.
> *Cheryl:* Talk about that prompt some more.
> *Amy:* I like that prompt because Tekwan gets fixated on his mis-
> take.
> *Cheryl:* Go ahead, talk about what happened.
> *Amy:* I was trying to get through that fix but he clearly wanted
> to be in control.
> *Cheryl:* What did we just learn about Tekwan?
> *Wendy:* He was excited about what he wrote.

These interactions show the teachers thinking about the nature of
the interactions and their implications, and making their thinking
public. It is within these conversations that they begin to internalize
agentive ways of talking and thinking about the interactions. Although Cheryl often prompts the teachers to comment, she does not
evaluate their comments. When she does respond it is normally to ask
for more comment, but more commonly other teachers provide further
commentary or extension. There is, of course, more to the interactions
than her verbal prompts. She does a lot of nodding with her head, and
she takes a nonauthoritarian stance, for example, leaning on a chair
with her foot on the seat or leaning comfortably on a wall, avoiding
direct eye contact with the person speaking, and looking to others to
extend the conversation.

Teachers regularly comment on this part of the class as very important in their development as keen observers of children. For example, in her reflective essay Jillian commented:

> The video and audio portions of the course were very useful. I learned a lot from watching the videos and having my colleagues critique me. I noticed things about myself such as over-relying on one strategy as well as the level of engagement of the learner. I saw teachable moments that I otherwise would have missed. Through watching and listening to myself I believe that I grew as an observer.

Through the videotaped discussions, the teachers have an opportunity to see a wide range of students and interactional styles. They also see a range of segments of instruction. If several teachers choose similar segments, such as book introductions, we approach the next teacher and ask if he or she would be comfortable choosing a different segment to present.

Teachers report learning from the videos about different instructional strategies, but also about the range of students. For example, Christine's responses focused on exactly these insights:

> The video is one of the highlights of this class. Not only viewing mine, but others, helped me to notice new things about the students and about the types of prompts I was giving. We learned from the good and the bad of each person's video and got the experience of working with different types of learners in a short amount of time.

The videotaped experiences also lead the teachers to more specific and more detailed observations of their teaching practices. In Tina's excerpt, she analyzes her lesson and considers the areas of her teaching that need reconsideration.

> After watching the tape I realized that I was dedicating too much time to reading and not enough time to writing. In fact, the day I videotaped I did not do any writing with Jeremiah. I also noticed that the prompts I used needed to be clearer and my praise needed to be more specific. I also noticed that I engaged Jeremiah in a conversation about the text instead of interrogating him about it.

The conversations around the videos take time to develop. They involve acquiring a new discourse, from noticing the significant behaviors and patterns to framing them in a way that will produce productive learning. In Chapter 9, Cheri Collisson examines the learning value of these video analyses.

TOOL 16. ANALYZING TRANSCRIPTS: RETHINKING THE LANGUAGE OF INTERACTIONS

Although the teachers are getting regular feedback from instructors and peers after their lessons and after their videotaped sessions, it is necessary that the teachers also learn to give themselves this feedback. To develop this competence, we have students analyze audio- and videotapes of their own teaching. In these transcript analyses teachers apply the knowledge they have gained and analytical understandings they have acquired. For example, consider the following analytic comments:

> I had commented in the previous transcription that, "I was responsible for initiating conversation about the text nearly 100% of the time." During this session I see myself transferring this control and responsibility over to Khareem. I took control initially by reintroducing the book to Khareem. Though I started with a question, "Do you remember what the alligator's name is?" Khareem was not yet interested in responding . . . My guiding question was weak and did not allow for much thinking to take place or a conversation to develop. However, the prompt "she has gotten into some trouble already" sparked Khareem's interest and memory about a specific event in the story. Throughout the rest of the reading experience, Khareem initiated 100% of the conversations about the story (6 in total)! This is incredible development!
>
> My goal has been to encourage Khareem to cross check in figuring out unfamiliar words . . . His monitoring is becoming second nature and I think naturally includes some cross checking. I did praise his work in these cases by saying "good self correct" and "nice job fixing words." However, I did fail at giving appropriate cross checking cues when he could not or did not self correct.
>
> There were three instances in which Khareem misread a word that affected meaning and I did not say anything. [specifies

words] . . . In particular, I should have encouraged him further on the *they* for *that* miscue because he noticed something wasn't right. [gives evidence] . . . I could have asked him if *they* looked right and made sense in the sentence. This would have demonstrated both visual and meaning based checking. I know he would have gotten it easily if I drew his attention to it again . . .

Though some teachers prefer the audiotape and some prefer the videotape, almost all find this analysis of their language choices and teaching practices particularly helpful. For example, Amy noted in her reflective essay at the end of the semester:

The ability to observe myself teaching through the use of the audiotapes and videotape helped me to see what worked and what did not. It was very powerful to see myself engaging in conversations with Tekwan and prompting him on many levels. And, it was humbling when I saw myself not follow his lead, stick to my agenda, and use a technique that was not the most effective. After analyzing my work in this way, I became very comfortable with abandoning things that were not working and not feeling like a failure if it did not turn out the way I had planned.

At the same time as providing productive reflective analysis, these transcriptions provide us, as instructors, a useful ground for additional conversations about the teachers' interactions with their students. Furthermore, the process of selecting a piece to transcribe, analyze, and share in itself is a useful reflective act.

LAYERS OF REFLECTIVE PRACTICE

Students *become* literate with all that entails about personhood, relationships, and values (Fairclough, 1992; Gee, 1996). We draw our teachers' attention to their impact on this process of becoming, and the discursive means through which they shape students' literate lives. We also draw their attention to the discursive contexts and histories that shape their practices—including our own conscious efforts to influence their practice, and the cultural threads that leave their unconscious mark. We do this so that they may responsibly inquire into their own practice and its development, and build their own self-extending systems.

However, we are also well aware of the parallel demands in our own practice. Our teachers are in the process of *becoming* teachers, and we expect that our interactions with them will impact the narrative structuring of their teaching identities. This requires that we apply the same principles of reflective practice to our own work. Our collaborative practice has been one important tool for extending our reflective practice, as has the writing of this book.

The next chapter, by Vanessa la Raé, shows how, through her reflective practice, she developed her understanding and teaching of genre, text difficulty, and critical literacy. She also shows her transfer of these understandings to her teaching of college students.

14

"You Brought Easy Books to Read Today. Hallelujah! Praise the Lord!"

VANESSA LA RAÉ

Every summer for the past several years, I have taught a graduate course entitled *Literature for Reading Programs.* In this course we study differences among a wide array of children's literature—the familiar, the less visible, new and developing genre practices, and the significance of diversity. We also examine student participation in book selection. My primary concern is with the books teachers will purchase, select, and use as they help students become independent readers and writers.

While many experiences continue to inform my instruction in this course, tutoring in the Literacy Lab was fundamental. It was there—in relationship with my peers, professors, assigned readings, and, most especially, the company of one student—that I learned important lessons about books. Thus, my goal for this chapter is to revisit what I learned in the Literacy Lab, to share how I came to understand what qualifies as the literature for reading programs, and where I have taken this learning.

MEETING LASHANDRA

In my third year as a doctoral student at the University at Albany, State University of New York, I enrolled in the Literacy Lab where I tutored a student throughout the spring semester. As is often the case for teachers, I read about my student LaShandra before I met her. The two-dimensional paper representation of her life described her as an African American child living in foster care. Almost 9 years of age, LaShandra was the oldest student in her second-grade classroom at a private Catholic school. She came to the lab because her classroom teacher suggested that "help in phonics" would enable her to "decode high frequency words."

In person, LaShandra was a slight child with a large smile and an abundance of conversational and physical energy. She shared many stories about her family and friends while moving about the room to touch books and write, draw, and erase on the chalkboard. Though I came to understand some of these behaviors as rooted in avoidance of reading and writing, her level of energy was a natural extension of her personality and desire to perform.

Preparing to work with LaShandra, I collected approximately 35 picture and chapter books, mostly realistic fiction. As part of "roaming in the known" (Clay, 1993b), I invited LaShandra to choose a book to read. She commenced her search in earnest, and her selection strategies were simple. She briefly examined the book cover and then flipped through the first few pages of text, casting aside books that did not meet her standards. I watched the growing pile of rejects presently accompanied by a chant of, "No," "No," and "No." After some 25 vetoes, LaShandra paused, smiled, and emerged with the book *A Chair for My Mother* by Vera Williams (1983). Turning to me, she exclaimed, "You brought easy books to read today. Hallelujah! Praise the Lord!"

STUDENT PARTICIPATION IN THE BOOK SELECTION PROCESS

A Chair for My Mother turned out to be LaShandra's "favorite book of all time." The story features a young girl named Rosa, her mother, and her grandmother. They want to buy a big, soft, comfortable chair for their apartment after losing all their furniture in a fire. First, however, they must save up all of their spare coins in a big glass jar. These spare coins come from the tips Rosa's mother earns as a waitress and the money saved by her grandmother when she finds a bargain at the market.

LaShandra borrowed this book several times, and requested tutoring time to read it aloud. Her enthusiasm never wavered, and it was obvious in listening to her read that this book held a deeply cherished story. Like LaShandra, most of us have favorite books we feel comfortable reading and books we are comforted by reading. As teachers, we want these for our students: favorite books, interesting books, comforting books, and books that will make our students want to read more.

When I teach *Literature for Reading Programs,* I am reminded of my initial book experience with LaShandra. I hear the relief in her voice, in her "Hallelujah! Praise the Lord!" As a direct result of that experience, I ask my teachers, "What role do students have in determining the literature of reading programs?"

Acknowledging that many children have a favorite book or favorite stories raises the question of what it means to collect books for, and share stories with, children before meeting or becoming acquainted with them. Children do read and hear many stories without ever participating in the book selection process. In many instances, this makes sense because teacher-selected texts are often appropriate, interesting, and necessary for instruction. Frequently, the books that teachers choose support the content or trajectory of the curriculum, are personal favorites, and are recognized as "good books" for children. Nonetheless, LaShandra's rejection of nearly every book I brought still forces me, and thus the teachers I work with, to involve children in the literature selection process, and increase the likelihood of finding books they will want to read or hear.

When I create the course syllabus for *Literature for Reading Programs,* determining the books, stories, poems, and so forth, I apply the same principles for the teachers. I invite them into the book selection process by asking, "How do you select your books? What do you like to read? What have you always wanted to read? What will you, or have you never, read?"

These questions lead to the selection of texts that later become the basis of small- and large-group book discussions. In addition, all teachers read a requisite number of books from established categories such as award-winning literature and multicultural literature. However, the books teachers elect to read to fulfill course requirements are always a matter of their own choosing. Because teachers are involved in the selection process both individually and collectively, my hope is that they will have a better sense of their own empowerment and their ability to effect change (Freire & Macedo, 1987; Luke & Gore, 1992). By participating in the book selection process, they then pass on the sense of empowerment to their students.

The issues involved in helping in-service professionals select the literature for reading programs have become more complex. The adoption of specific reading programs by school districts means fewer and fewer opportunities for teacher choice, let alone student choice. The teachers and I will have to reimagine ways to include students in the book selection process and to incorporate children's home and community literacy practices as part of the literacy curriculum.

EASY BOOKS AND LEVELING TEXTS

While LaShandra's comment of "You brought easy books to read today" signaled something significant about my book selection process, it also caused me to think more carefully about the notion of "easy books." Not only was *A Chair for My Mother* (1983) a special book, but it was also a book that LaShandra could read. She had memorized the story and the words. While reading, she gave as much attention to watching me listen to her read as she did to the print. Her obvious interest was in proving to me that she was a reader.

In that first meeting, LaShandra's search proceeded from her own predetermined criteria. She could distinguish the "easy books" from the presumably "hard books." An "easy book" meant a familiar text she could read, and that allowed her to demonstrate her identity of "reader" to me, her new audience. Although LaShandra distinguished "easy books" from "hard books," gaining access to "easy books" was not guaranteed in her school experience. I learned, after visiting LaShandra's classroom, that many of the assigned books and stories were well above her reading level. This likely meant that for the first 4 months of school and until she joined the Literacy Lab, her classroom reading experiences were unsuccessful and frustrating, spent in texts beyond her zone of proximal development.

Knowledge and use of appropriately leveled texts was important for affording LaShandra opportunities to develop a self-extending system for reading. This also required a greater balance in her use of semantic, syntactic, and grapho-phonemic cueing systems. When she first came to the Literacy Lab, she estimated unknown words based on initial and ending letters, often not preserving meaning. For example, in the sentence "Annie is a sad girl," LaShandra read the word *said* for *sad*. Manageable and meaningful texts were central for this shift toward making meaning. Guided Reading (Fountas & Pinnell, 1999) levels J and K books were LaShandra's instructional level, and she expressed interest in the series *Nate the Great,* reading *Nate the Great* (Sharmat, 1977) and *Nate the Great and the Boring Beach Bag* (Sharmat, 1989). The familiar characters (Nate, Rosamond, Sludge, etc.) and predictable storylines (something is lost or missing, the search for clues) helped LaShandra learn to figure out unknown words by asking: "What would make sense there?" Because of this experience, when I teach *Literature for Reading Programs,* I introduce teachers to the practice of leveling texts through the guidelines offered by Fountas and Pinnell (1996), providing teachers with a generally stable and beginning reference from which to match books to readers. A challenge involves the balance of presenting high-interest content while maintaining a manageable reading level. This is especially important when working with children in the upper end of elementary school and in the middle and upper grades. These readers are apt to lean toward more sophisticated content either as indicative of their individual preferences or as required by the school curriculum. Reading material that is too difficult will be rejected, as are texts perceived as too immature.

READING PREFERENCES AND GENRES

As a teacher in the Literacy Lab, one of the first things I learned was to recognize and honor children's established literacy practices and preferences. From our initial meeting it was clear that LaShandra's motivation for finding a book she could read stemmed from her own reading and life interests. LaShandra preferred to read poetry, especially poems with a certain cadence, rhythm, and repetition, and when she read poetry, the words became encoded on her body. She kept pace with the syncopation of the words by nodding her head, tapping her foot, rocking in her chair, clapping, and changing the pitch, intensity, and duration of the words and phrases. She didn't just read: she performed the poem. She requested that poetry reading be included in each tutoring session, and "The Animal Song" (Evans, 1997) became her favorite poem. Eventually her fluency practice included self-selected poems from *Soap Soup and Other Verses* (Kushkin, 1999), *A Light in the Attic* (Silverstein, 1981), *New Kid on the Block* (Prelutsky, 1984), *Honey, I Love and Other Poems* (Greenfield, 1978) and *Soul Looks Back in Wonder* (Feelings, 1993).

As part of the final celebration, LaShandra read poetry selections to her peers, other teachers, and members of the school community. At home, according to her foster mother, LaShandra read her poetry selections to friends and family. By selecting poems and reading them aloud, she began to acknowledge herself as a "good reader," a literate identity previously missing from her self-descriptive repertoire. Establishing this foothold or "comfort zone" with poetry allowed me to nudge her toward other genres: mysteries, nonfiction, and biography.

Recalling how important it was to recognize and establish time for LaShandra to read poetry and then expand her reading in new directions has informed my teaching of *Literature for Reading Programs* in several ways. We discuss, for example, why poetry reading is often absent from the classroom routine and curriculum. Poetry is a well-known example because despite its many possibilities, it remains underutilized in the language arts curriculum (Perfect, 1999). Throughout the semester, teachers and I gather to read and share poems. This includes locating collections within and beyond the predictable poetry canon. Over the years, in-class readings have ranged from the familiar, humorous work of Shel Silverstein, Jack Prelutsky, and Kalli Dakos to the poignant, uplifting, and spiritual poetry of Maya Angelou, Langston Hughes, Arnold Adoff, Joseph Bruchac, and Nikki Grimes to the painful, haunting, and disturbing images portrayed in poetry and poetry memoir by Eirann Corrigan, Carolyn Forche, Marie Howe, and Wislawa Szymborska. Other contributions include *My Man Blue* (Grimes, 1999), *Harlem* (Myers, 1997), *Smoky Night* (Bunting, 1999), *The Palm of My Heart* (Adedjouma, 1996), *Nappy Hair* (Herron, 1997), and *The House That Crack Built* (Taylor, 1992).

As with some of the poetry LaShandra read, these poems and verses focus on images of history and social inequality, and on accurately restoring the many voices and lives of silenced minorities. Because of these poems and many others, the teachers begin to acknowledge the abundance of possibilities for connections to critical literacy and social justice—areas not normally in their comfort zones. Teachers tend to gravitate toward what they like and what they know. In class, moving teachers beyond their comfort zone with regard to genre begins with a few informal surveys (raise your hand). The teachers (virtually all white, female, and middle-class) like and populate their classroom libraries with a great deal of realistic fiction and historical fiction. For example, fifth-grade teachers have often explained how *Letters from Rifka* (Hesse, 1992) supports the powerful ideas generated by the topic of immigration within the social studies curriculum. Overwhelmingly, they remain eager to read realistic fiction and historical fiction such as *Money Hungry* (Flake, 2001), *Tangerine* (Bloor, 2001), *Stuck in Neutral* (Trueman, 2000), *A Single Shard* (Park, 2001), *The Art of Keeping Cool* (Lisle, 2000), and *Out of the Dust* (Hesse, 1997).

When the assigned text genres are fantasy and science fiction, there is not the same excited sense of "I can't wait to read this book." With the exception of a few familiar low fantasy stories such as the *Harry Potter* series (Rowling, 1998), *Charlotte's Web* (White, 1952), and *Poppy* (Avi, 1997), fantasy is not a favored text genre. Neither is science fiction, which they tend to equate with *Star Trek*, *Star Wars*, or violent video games. They have little experience with fantasy, science, graphic novels, or manga (Japanese comics), all text genres that some children select for their leisure reading.

Just as we were nudged in the Literacy Lab to stretch beyond our comfort zones, I nudge teachers toward these unfamiliar genres. We read *Ender's Game* (Card, 1977), *Among the Hidden* (Haddix, 1998), *Artemis Fowl* (Coifer, 2001), and *The Last Book in the Universe* (Philbrick, 2000). Teachers are quick to note the many instructional opportunities that such text genres afford. For example, science fiction texts frequently address issues related to war, social conditions, and technology, introducing science and social studies content knowledge and opening spaces for critical literacy practices. Similar observations can be made regarding nonfiction texts.

But of course there are also books that challenge simple genre categories, such as *The Three Little Pigs* (Weisner, 2001), *Black and White* (McCauley, 1990), and *Re-Zoom* (Banyai, 1998). These books are constructed to defy the presumptions of known text genres. In these postmodern texts, where the only given is that nothing is a foregone conclusion, one can find animals flying in and out of fairy tales, print falling off the page, uneven font, and words printed in circles. These books with multiple text genres and ones that break the conventions of known text genres are excellent for introducing and developing critical literacy practices. Such books are ideal for questioning the author or illustrator's intent, the role of a reader, and the power of text and illustrations. New genre practices continue to emerge. Manga, game manuals, and comics once occupied a small section of a single bookshelf. They now take up entire sections of bookstores. Part of my time this semester will be spent inviting teachers to explore this literature. While it is helpful to think about text genres as a beginning point for discussion and inclusion, this perspective on genre is overly simplistic. Even text genres, such as realistic fiction, fantasy, and science fiction, are not immutable categories. LaShandra's initial reading of poems aloud to me, her family, and friends suggests how text genres are linked to social practices. Text genres are articulated by what teachers and students do with texts and are better theorized as genre practices (Kamberelis, 1999). My question to teachers—"What are the genres absent from the curriculum?"—is one that unfolds over the course of the semester. In *Literature for Reading,* we begin by identifying text as genres and look for what is missing in our classrooms but yet is evident in children's literate lives. Over the course of the semester, teachers come to view this question as less about text as genre and more about what genre practices are absent in classrooms. Teachers recognize that genres are never as absolute as they are generally defined.

Teachers' understandings change as we write, think, and talk about the many ways books are read, handled, and discussed.

REPRESENTING WHO WE ARE

LaShandra rejoiced in the book *A Chair for My Mother* (Williams, 1983) because of the appeal in the message this story held for her. I suspected then, as I do now, that this story told about a life that she knew, had lived, or in some way had experienced. It spoke to her on a personal level. We all have favorite stories, books, and characters that resonate with some aspect of our lives. For me that occurs in the character of Stella in *Stella, Star of the Sea, Stella, Queen of the Snow*, and *Stella, Fairy of the Forest* (Gay, 1999, 2000, 2002). I am drawn to Stella's adventures in nature, her patient and impatient treatment of her sibling, her wild red hair, and her big, round belly. Though Stella was created long after my childhood, in ways most apparent, she and I have a great deal in common.

We all need to experience stories that connect with who we are or might become. These are the stories that recognize and affirm something important, even vital, about our lives, that speak to the many ways we have of being in the world, that represent and thereby honor our many possible life experiences. These are the stories that recall who we were, who we are, and who we might become. Although children may not always choose stories based on a personal sense of recognition or connection to a character, plot, or theme, similar indexes of their life experiences must be part of the available, privileged literature.

Despite a utopian tendency to believe otherwise, it is still true that certain histories, certain stories, certain lifestyles, and the possibility of many selves are absent from the reading programs, collections, and canons of literature students are asked to read. It is not surprising—given the tight control exercised by the publishing industry, and the societal tensions over issues such as gay marriage, religious freedom, personal choice, and freedom of speech—that children's everyday lives are largely absent from the literature they are asked to read.

In my first meeting with LaShandra the books I offered her were based on my preconceived notions about what she would like or need to read. That LaShandra was a child of color living in the city and in foster care weighed heavily in determining the books I presented to her. My choices for LaShandra included books such as *Meet Danitra*

Brown (Grimes, 1994), *Come On Rain!* (Hesse, 1999), *Amazing Grace* (Hoffman, 1991), *Tar Beach* (Ringold, 1991), and *The Great Gilly Hopkins* (Paterson, 1978). If LaShandra had been interested in stories about children of color living in the city and in foster care, finding such descriptions was not impossible. However, locating books about the lives of children of color and other nonmainstream social indexes is never as easy as finding books about white, middle-class social identities and lives.

In *Literature of Reading Programs,* the topic of representation in children's literature undergirds many course readings, presentations, classroom activities, and large- and small-group discussions. One of the liveliest conversations proceeds from acknowledging who and what have been ignored by the publishing industry. I ask teachers, "Who was missing from your books?" and "Who or what did you want to read about but never could find?" The examples offered are quite revealing. Teachers—even white, middle-class teachers—recall that as children their books had almost no redheads; kids with braces; bald kids; kids in wheelchairs; kids with pimples, birthmarks, or moles; overweight kids; or kids with lisps, cleft palate scars, or back braces. Absent from the literature were the children with hearing aids, thick corrective lenses, albinism, cerebral palsy, cystic fibrosis, and mental handicaps—unless of course the story was only about the handicapping condition, such as *I Have a Sister, My Sister Is Deaf* (Whitehouse, 1977).

There were few, if any, main characters who were African American, Native American, Hispanic American, Asian American, Indian, Middle Eastern, and so forth. Common cultural names like Huan Yue, Jiang Li, Yaholo, Ahmed, Syir, Ja-Quasha, Iratxo, Jaya, Raja, Yana, Pilar, Se'Quar, Hari, or Jamil never appeared in stories. All the children were gendered because the notion of a transgendered child didn't (and still doesn't) exist in the literature. Quite predictably, gender stereotypes prevailed; few of the girls were leaders, smart, and athletic, and none of the boys ever appeared as domestic and nurturing.

Not only were certain kinds of kids and identities not present in the literature, but neither were certain family structures: for example, single parent and multigenerational families, foster families, stepfamilies, blended families, and adoptive families. With regard to plot and setting, the storylines and social conditions in which textbook children lived out their lives were decidedly white, middle-class, and suburban. There was no literature representing other customs, races, nationalities, creeds, and religions. The joy/celebration of harvest, prayer, pilgrimage, festival, coming of age, menstruation, worship, meditation, consumption, marriage, birth, and death were notably absent from the literature. Similarly, the negative conditions in which children must sometimes live their lives—such as child abuse, poverty, neglect, abandonment, violence, alcoholism, divorce, and murder—were also not regularly available storylines to which children could turn to read.

Over the last 30 years or so, there has been some notable improvement with regard to representation. Authors such as Crews, Draper, Hamilton, Hesse, Johnson, Keats, Lester, McKissack, Myers, and Steptoe write authentic stories about children of color, their lives, and their many experiences. In *Literature for Reading Programs*, we discuss and write about the powerful use of language and illustrations these authors choose, focusing on the importance of setting, history, and circumstance, and the reflection of diversity.

Despite the increased inclusion of once-marginalized voices in children's literature, there still exist many unresolved questions of representation related to the social indexes of gender, race, and class, to name a few. The teachers (and I) view this as an unresolved tension, but one that provides an opportunity for critical conversation both within the college classroom and within elementary and secondary classrooms.

New challenges have developed as a result of the introduction of critical literacy practices into the school curriculum. One of the goals of a socially responsive curriculum is helping teachers and students become more comfortable with the discomfort that occurs in acknowledging a nation's history and in accurately representing the diversity found throughout society. Literature can provide the grounds for such work, but only if such literature continues to be published. Decreases in the number of publishing companies and increases in the overall control of the publishing industry have made it difficult to find "culturally conscious" texts (Sims-Bishop, 1983). Not only must the literature of reading programs be culturally conscious, it should also include narratives that focus on issues of social justice. Further, the inclusion of critical literacy practices as part of a socially responsive curriculum becomes especially tricky when books children prefer to read, enjoy, and share reinforce sexist, classist, or racist ideologies. As such, the literature of reading programs must consider to what degree such stereotypic ideologies are present. Here it is the responsibility of the reading educator to help children expand their reading in new directions. In conjunction with other reading practices, children must acquire the critical reading strategies that will allow them to recognize and read against sexist, racist, and classist ideologies.

In terms of these challenges, what may be required of reading teachers, classroom teachers, administrators, librarians, and even parents is an expanded search. School libraries, national bookstore chains, and school- and academic-sponsored book fairs represent several familiar avenues for exploration. Visiting privately owned bookstores and perusing independent publishing catalogues offer other possibilities for finding high-interest/low-difficulty texts. Nontraditional texts (i.e., children's magazines, picture books, newspapers, comics, online articles, and student-authored works) yield an even greater range of choices for capturing and maintaining the interest of readers at all levels.

A FEW FINAL WORDS

What I brought to my initial meetings in the Literacy Lab with La-Shandra was a set of unexamined assumptions. I assumed that I knew what books would be good for her. I assumed that I knew what reading practices would extend her literate proficiencies. I assumed that I knew *her*. Working with LaShandra forced me to examine each of these assumptions. I quickly came to see how each of these preexisting expectations were less about her and more about me and what I believed to be true about her as a literacy learner. Thus, an important first step toward changing the direction of our tutoring sessions was to recognize and acknowledge my assumptions. The discussions I had with my peers, careful observations, and acknowledging who LaShandra was all helped me to abandon my preexisting expectations for LaShandra and involve her in the learning process. I came to recognize and value her practices. I then used those understandings and appreciations as a basis for extending her literacy practices in new, expansive directions.

As I prepare for another semester teaching *Literature for Reading Programs,* one in which the students and I will read, discuss, and evaluate hundreds of books, I am reminded of LaShandra and her "Hallelujah!" and "You brought easy books" comments. I remain mindful of the importance of student choice and providing students with access to a range of texts. Such mindfulness begins with acknowledging who my students are and valuing what literacy and genre practices they bring to the table.

As a reflective practitioner, I continue to explore new ways to discuss text genres and genre practices and to think about these issues in more complex ways. I am aware of the introduction of critical literacy and the need for a more socially responsive curriculum, especially as it applies to the issue of representation in literature. That means helping students think about continually evolving ways of including others in their classroom curriculum. This requires that the students and I act as co-authors in the construction of the syllabus and the content of the conversations. I hope that the teachers will carry their experiences forward to their students as they jointly determine what qualifies as the literature of reading programs.

Part III

TEACHER CHANGE
AND PROGRAM CHANGE

This final section of the book considers teacher change and the evolution of the program. Although we have described and provided examples of teacher development throughout the book, in chapter 15 we examine the indicators we use to evaluate the effects of our teaching and their basis. In the final chapter, chapter 16, we pull together the threads of the book, describe our current problem-solving, and present a prospective look at the trajectory of our work.

15

Dimensions and Markers of Teacher Change

In this chapter, we summarize the dimensions of change we look for in our teachers and the markers we use to document that change. Teacher development—conceptual, practical, and relational—is complex and often subtle. Though we do strive for the development of technical skills, they are of limited help without deeper changes. The desire to understand the learner and the ability to create situations in which the learner will be successful requires caring and respect. The teachers must develop a sense of themselves and their student, and a relationship of care. The relationship between teacher and student is what mediates the ways in which the student understands the teacher's interactions. For example, following the student's lead and imagining the student's logic require teachers to decenter—to actually find the student interesting. This means not focusing on themselves or turning teaching into an ego-involving activity (Nicholls, 1989). Similarly, teachers who enter with a judgmental sensibility must lose it, particularly with regard to linguistic and cultural values and practices.

Imagining the student's logic and point of view requires close observation of what the student does and says, and how he or she does and says it. This requires knowing what features are important to notice, and a personal commitment and respect that casts the logic in a productive light. Unless the teachers frame and structure activities so that students are successful, waiting for students to figure things out or to self-correct will be unproductive; and since the child will be unable to take control of the activity, following the child's lead will also be unproductive. These inferences will require imagining the activity from the child's perspective: both an act of will (error has to be seen as an opportunity to learn and an indicator of what is known) and of skill (the teacher has to imagine herself into the child's thinking—an act of social imagination). These dimensions are all thoroughly interconnected and reciprocal. Failure to respect the child's authority and agency will produce instructional relationships that invite resistance and limit engagement and the information available to inform instruction.

EVIDENCE FOR CHANGE

We require teachers to document their students' learning and their own. We also must look for evidence of the effectiveness of our own teaching practices. Fortunately, many of the tools we use as part of teaching simultaneously provide evidence of change. For example, transcripts from early and later in the semester offer not only a space for learning, but also evidence of it. Teachers reflect on these as part of their self-evaluation, and both sources of evidence are available to us.

In the next section we expand the connections between evidence and the complex learning we expect. As with assessment of any complex learning, all indicators are partial, and we resist reducing the learning to the indicator. We also depend on multiple indicators. We begin with the concept of conversational relationships, which underpins both our teaching and what we ask of our teachers. We then proceed to examine the central conceptual issue of following the child's lead and the associated strategic practices.

THOUGHTFUL CONVERSATIONS AND ACTIVE LISTENING

When we have been successful, observing our teachers is like listening in on a thoughtful conversation—a dialogue. Teaching sessions generally do not begin that way. Initially, the teachers are often caught up in the things they have to teach and what they have planned, and they bring to their teaching a delivery system epistemology in which they use technical skills to impart their knowledge to their student. Underlying this approach is also a deficit framing of the student; the teachers often suspect that perhaps the student has nothing to say or will be unable to solve the problem they face. This is not lost on the students. Framing interactions through this epistemology positions the child as having no authority and does not convey a message of respect. We look for a shift toward a more symmetrical relationship.

Symmetrical Relationships

In the following book introduction from the second half of the semester, Nikki, a teacher, and Tekwan, a third-grader, engage in an instructional conversation where they are both positioned as learners. In this interaction, Nikki learns about Tekwan's interests, connections he makes prior to reading the text, and the strategies he uses when he encounters unknown words. The dynamic nature of the conversation leads to Tekwan's interest and engagement in the text.

Nikki: Today we are going to start reading the book that you chose, *Triplet Trouble and the Field Day Disaster* [Dadey & Jones, 1996]. Can you tell me why you chose this book?

Tekwan: I like sports.

Nikki: Will this be about sports?

Tekwan: Yes.

Nikki: How do you know?

Tekwan: The kid on the front is jumping in a contest.

Nikki: Good! Does Douglass Elementary have a field day?

Tekwan: Yes, we all go out and run against the whole third grade.

Nikki: What is your favorite event at field day?

Tekwan: I like to race because I am really fast.

Nikki: Okay, there will some words we need to look at before we read. The first word is on this page. Can you find the word *compete*?

Tekwan: (points to the word)

Nikki: How do you know?

Tekwan: I found the longer *c* word.

Nikki: Good! In this sentence it says, "We get to compete in all kinds of games." What does *compete* mean here?

Tekwan: Like to play against people, you know, like racing against people.

Nikki: Excellent! The next word is *brilliant*, and it is on this page.

Tekwan: (again points to the word)

Nikki: And how do you know that?

Tekwan: I can see the word *ill* in it.

Nikki: Good, so you are seeing the chunks again.

Tekwan: Uh-huh.

Nikki: So what does that mean? Can you read the sentence and figure out the word?

Tekwan: I know *brilliant* means smart.

Nikki: How do you know that without reading the sentence?

Tekwan: Grandma says, "Me, I'm brilliant."

Nikki: Well, let's read it, and see if it means the same thing.

Tekwan: (reading from text) "Alex had another one of her big ideas." It means the same thing.

Nikki: Good, one more word. It's *lassoing*, and it is on this page.

Tekwan: (points to *lassoing*) I don't know.

Nikki: Well, they're talking about a rope and making a loop out of it, so what could it be?

Tekwan: Like the cowboys.

Nikki: Good, they lasso the cows.

Tekwan: We see that sometimes on the TV.

Nikki: Good! Let's start reading.

In this transcript Nikki shows her anticipation of areas of potential difficulty and her twin emphases on what Tekwan brings to reading and how he figures things out. These emphases make it possible for Tekwan to be in control of his reading, and help him explain his strategic actions. The balanced relationship is indicated by the similar volume of talk and by the shared control of conversational topic. Still later in the semester we will expect a reduction in the evaluative language ("good," "excellent"), which maintains an element of asymmetry.

Opening Dialogue

Actually having a conversation with a child is a major obstacle for many teachers to begin with. The primary interactional tools many bring are questions. Questions are commonly very controlling interaction strategies, particularly because they insist on a response and they control the expected nature of the response. They are particularly controlling if they are closed questions—questions that have a single correct answer. Teachers also begin with the idea that comprehension instruction and assessment happens at the end of a story, and requires asking questions to ensure that the child has gotten the meaning. These changes show up in transcripts, but also in reflective writing. For example, Anna writes in her reflective essay of the changes in her teaching and questioning through working with Hassad, a first-grader:

> During and after reading, Hassad often commented as to why I was asking him so many questions. I was checking for comprehension and trying to engage him in conversation around the

story. Not until taking a close look at the language I was using did I realize that I was interrogating Hassad, not engaging in conversation. I looked back through my instructional logs and found that I was asking him questions that required a literal, one word answer. My questions were not open-ended, therefore, conversation was not taking place. Over the semester, questions became open-ended or were framed as statements that changed interrogation into conversation. For example, "What was the mistake the character made?" changed to "Tell me how you would've handled the situation differently if you were the character." The new language that I was using encouraged Hassad to think beyond the book, beyond the literal, and to make connections between the story world and his world and his experiences.

Conversational Teaching

In the early classes, teachers learn to use certain prompts to guide instruction. Initially they use the prompts in a static and inflexible manner, for example, "Does that make sense?" "Does that sound right?" "What letters would you expect to be there?" "Does it look right?" "How could you check?" (Clay, 1993b). They do not build these into natural ongoing conversations. As teachers develop their expertise, these prompts become integrated into ongoing instructional conversations. We see this in our observations as interactions become more conversational. The teachers see it, too. As Erica noted,

> When I first began tutoring, prompting Khaleem to use all three cueing systems felt alien to me. Every phrase and prompt felt forced, and now those phrases and prompts feel like second nature. Verbalizing exactly what strategy Khaleem used and praising him for his work started off as awkward.

Teachers' increasingly sophisticated use of language as an instructional tool develops a better conceptual understanding of literacy acquisition in general, and of an individual student's development in particular. An aspect that complicates this development is the ongoing teaching experience of the teachers. For example, teachers who are teaching while they take the class have ongoing opportunities to practice their use of instructional language—albeit with a different age group. Teachers who lack this ongoing experience find it much more difficult. For them, flexibility is slower to come.

Wait Time

For many teachers this wait is very difficult. For example, in one of our research projects (Dozier, Johnston, & Delsanto, 2001) involving three case studies of middle school struggling readers, all three teachers acknowledged from their audiotaped analysis at the beginning of the semester that they provided little wait time, pointing out that they even answered their own questions if their student remained silent. Later in the semester, their analysis of a second audiotape showed a change in this pattern. For example, in one of these transcripts Sarah's wait times ranged from 2 to 4 seconds. Not only that, Sarah recognized that when she provided time for her student to respond, he opened up the conversation in unexpected ways. Because it is difficult to make this change, initially some of our teachers have to consciously count in their heads to prevent themselves from interrupting. This use of silent speech as a tool to manage behavior is useful, but ultimately this conscious control becomes unnecessary when the teachers come to understand that what the children have to say is valuable and to understand the significance of having students in control of their learning.

FOLLOWING THE STUDENT'S LEAD

For productive instructional interactions to happen, we believe that selecting an activity that is accessible and relevant to the student is the first order of business. Failure to accomplish this produces several problems. If children persist in trying to participate in inaccessible activities, it will lead to a set of interactions in which the child is a secondary participant and in which failure and negative responses are common, both of which are part of what children learn. Most importantly, the child cannot take control of the activity without redefining it in problematic ways, often as a contest for control.

For students to be in control of their learning the teacher must select accessible activities or make inaccessible ones accessible. Learning to manage the accessibility of activities requires choice of texts, activities, and topics, as well as choices in the way language is used to mediate difficulty through book introductions and ongoing conversations. Managing this consistently takes some time.

Evidence of effective management of instructional activities is found in running records and sheer volume of writing. It is also evident in the ratio of teacher to child contributions in the transcripts, as we saw with Tekwan and Nikki. It is also often observable from a distance in the relative body positions of teacher and student.

Even when the task is accessible, if it is not relevant children might still have no interest in taking control of their learning, particularly if they see the risks of taking control as too great. They actually have to see that it is in their short-term interest to engage in the activity. In other words, difficulty is affected by *intention* as well as by the structural demands of the activity (Holdaway, 1979). Our teachers have to learn how to select materials and activities that the children will find engaging that involve cultural and personal knowledge.

Arranging for the child to lead also requires the teacher to adopt a particular stance toward the child. It requires encouraging, but not forcing, the child to take control. It is common at first for teachers, aware that they need to arrange for the child to take the lead, to attempt to force the student to do so when they meet resistance. This move can turn the interactions into a destructive control game that does damage to the relationship, among other things. Negotiating control is a delicate balance, particularly for students who have not had a history of success or of being in control of their learning. It is best that children take control by invitation. For example, teachers can increase access by sharing the reading of the books with the student or by taking turns with the reading, thus modeling the use of expression, taking on the voices of different characters, and so forth. However, the teacher needs to remain mindful that the more extensive the support, the greater the risk that children will not be or feel in control of the activity. Knowing when and how to provide a necessary nudge so that a child gains the experience of success is central but also subtle.

In this excerpt from her reflective essay, Kendra, a teacher, points to her changes in following the lead of her learner, Asia:

> Prior to this course, my teaching experiences involved teacher-directed activities and questioning. I did not stop to think about my students' strengths or possible sources of confusions, nor did I allow them to make connections to their own lives. When working with Asia, I learned how to follow her lead. Often, our conversations allowed me to understand her prior knowledge of a specific topic and/or her own experiences. Those conversations helped me to make her learning more effective.

Kendra's comments illustrate her shift from a teacher-driven curriculum to her attention to her student's interests, understandings, and activities that allow the display of student strengths.

IMAGINING THE STUDENT'S LOGIC

Just as following the child's lead requires teachers (and us) to decenter, so does imagining the student's logic. It is an empathic process requiring not only an understanding of the child's knowledge, experience, culture and language, but also the will and care to engage in the imaginative act. Teachers must try to anticipate the student's likely reactions (cognitive, social, and emotional) to particular instructional strategies and materials. An active social imagination—expressed as sensitivity to such issues as participants' personal and learning histories, as well as to the developing relationship within the instructional sessions—is an important part of the teaching interaction.

Some of this need to understand the student's logic is evident when teachers explicitly ask students for reasoning related to errors and problem-solving. This becomes increasingly common as the semester unfolds, with the question often taking the form, "How did you know_____?" Some of the teachers' theorizing about students' understanding is also evident in less overt ways. For example, they regularly adjust book introductions around the difficulties they anticipate their students will encounter. These shifts are evident in their lesson logs, the transcripts, and in teachers' explanations of their instructional decision-making during community conversations and videotape analyses.

We look particularly for changes in teachers' responses to errors. At first, many of our teachers treat errors as a location for correction. Our goal is to have errors viewed as potential learning opportunities for teacher and student, not simply as behaviors to be corrected. There are three important ways in which teachers' perceptions and methods change in relation to their attention to errors. First, teachers come to regard errors as sources of information for learning for both teacher and student: as indicators of thinking in the zone of proximal development. Second, teachers move away from focusing on every error, instead bringing to a child's attention only those errors that will give a productive learning experience, given what is known about the child's development. Third, teachers shift their attention toward what Clay calls the "partially correct": that is, they attend first (and draw children's attention) to the part of the error that indicates productive reasoning. This is an act of teasing out confusions and clarifying incomplete concepts before extending the learning.

The wait time we have already discussed is one indicator of a teacher coming to view errors as opportunities to learn rather than as calls for correction or judgment (Dozier, Johnston, & Delsanto, 2001).

Another indicator is when teachers begin selectively ignoring and attending to particular errors. This shift can be seen in Meghan's teaching. Although she selected appropriate-level texts for her student, Julie, to read during the first sessions, she insisted on complete accuracy in the reading. By midway through the semester, observation showed that she was ignoring errors that did not offer an opportunity for productive problem-solving. In writing, too, rather than correcting errors during conferences, she attended more to what Julie, the writer, needed to learn. For example, when Julie was writing about her friend Dianne, a figure skater, Meghan—rather than pointing out the lack of detail in the writing—framed Julie's rereading of her piece with the comment: "You want to give enough detail so that someone reading your piece can picture her." This is an example of what Clay (1991a) would call "teaching for strategies."

Teachers' responses to students' accurate identification of words offer another indicator of the shift to treating students' errors as opportunities to learn. By midway through the semester, a student's correct identification of a problematic word was usually not the end of the instructional interaction. Instead, the teacher would extend the interaction by asking how the student had solved the problem or ask the student to cross-check the solution. If mere accurate performance were the goal, these responses would be beside the point. But with student learning as the goal, these responses reinforce the students' successful learning strategies and promote their independence as readers.

USING LANGUAGE AS A TOOL
FOR BUILDING AGENCY

The students our teachers tutor often do not see themselves as competent learners with respect to literacy. It is our teachers' job over the course of the semester to help students build productive identities that include a sense of agency in literate practices. For example, Billy, one of our students, described his growth as a reader over the course of the semester as follows: "Now when I read, I don't need my mom. Before I didn't like reading, but now I'm starting to like it." When Sarah asked him what he liked now, he answered, "I like the books. I like having the choice to pick the books." Appropriating his teacher's language, he added, "In school I raise my hand more and I don't mess up like I used to . . . I read for meaning. I try to find words I know inside other words." He also described reading strategies he had begun to use in his science class.

Agency and Identity

One part of the change in identity is the sense of authority built into dialogical interactions. However, we believe that teachers are also offering narrative possibilities within which students can locate themselves in agentive ways (Somers, 1994). For example, when Sarah says to Billy, "I notice you just self-corrected. How did you know to do that?" Billy relates a narrative, beginning with "I . . . " Sarah then follows his explanation with a prompt to identify a characteristic of the protagonist of his narrative: "That's what readers do." In other words, she invites him to recount an agentive narrative in which he includes himself as the active protagonist who identifies as a reader. This offering of an agentive role in the narrative develops in numerous ways in the interactions between these teachers and their students. For example, when the teacher reflects back to the student primarily what he or she did well, particularly in solving problems, the invitation is to construct a narrative in which the protagonist is active and successful. The intention is that the teachers' positive focus ultimately helps students notice, and own, their productive strategies, tilting their conceptions toward a more productive view of their competence, as we saw in Billy's comments.

Framing Literacy as Agentive

Another way in which agency plays an increasing role in the tutoring sessions is in the way literacy is presented in the discourse and activities of instruction. Literacy comes to be presented as an agentive activity, a central aspect of critical literacy. At the outset, for example, teachers as well as students often find it difficult to conceive of writing or reading as purposeful—as useful for something other than learning to read and write. This changes most noticeably because of the critical literacy emphasis in the class. Reading, too, becomes presented as more agentive as students learn to take a more active role in positioning themselves with respect to others. These changes can also be seen in teachers' nonacademic activities. For example, they report writing to their senators and newspapers, noticing gendered and racial dimensions of television programming, and noticing these dimensions in their personal reading.

In order to produce agentive narratives, children and teachers necessarily have to have taken the lead in solving problems. Telling a child, or a teacher, what to do and then having them do it defeats the possibility of constructing such a narrative. Encouraging a child to take the lead requires not only structuring an activity in a way that makes it possible for the child to successfully struggle, it requires offering sufficient time for that struggle to occur. Similarly, if children are to correct their own errors, they must have time and support to engage in the necessary conscious processing. This is no less true for teachers and teacher educators.

EVIDENCE OF DEEPER CHANGE

The challenge for our teachers is to learn to "follow the child's lead" without following it down unproductive paths. It is the timing, focus, positioning, prompting, invitation, and uptake of the teacher–student interactions that provide concrete markers of teachers' growing ability to meet the challenge. These markers provide us with feedback as to whether we are achieving our instructional goals. Since we make no secret of these indicators, teachers, too, are attending to them and to changes in them as they reflect on their teaching through videotape and audiotape analyses.

In the end, the complex changes we expect are underpinned by some fundamental changes in who teachers think they are, what they think they are doing, and who they think their students are. It is these changes that orchestrate real change in teachers' instruction and their ability to transfer their learning to other contexts (Dozier & Rutten, in press). A way to show this overall shift is through a second data poem. The first data poem, in chapter 1, showed teachers' thinking at the beginning of the semester in regard to literacy, language, and learning. The following data poem consists of excerpts from teachers' final reflective essays and provides a contrasting portrait.

> Knowing Children: Knowing Ourselves
> From the moment Tasha and I
> walked around her neighborhood,
> our relationship changed.
> Once I set aside my uncertainties and fears
> about talking about race as a white teacher,
> we ended up having great discussions.
> After I got to know his family,
> I made better decisions about my teaching.
> From working with families,
> I learned that we must stop making assumptions.
> I learned the importance of language
> and the strength of words.

Telling is not teaching.
I was interrogating my student,
not engaging in conversation.
I needed to stop intervening so much,
my constant questioning was interfering
with her fluency and comprehension.
Before I could teach Javon the language
he could use to develop a self-extending system,
I had to learn it for myself.
The responsibility to accelerate one student
is a tremendous undertaking.
Good teaching does not come from a book
or a prepackaged curriculum kit.
Good teaching comes from
following the lead of my learner.
I have grown,
both as a learner and as a teacher.

16

Evolution and Direction: Surprises, Dilemmas, and Unanswered Questions

At the outset we noted that it is our responsibility and privilege to teach teachers. It is also our responsibility and privilege to learn—to research and evolve our practice. The conceptual work we have begun in this book is, of course, never done. It is constantly evolving, which makes the course at once time-consuming, discomforting, and thoroughly engaging.

The histories teachers bring to our program reflect their schooling in a very uncritical literacy in a segregated society. Consequently, our tools are designed to disrupt these learning histories and help expand teachers' interest in the discomfort of learning and teaching a literacy of agency—a critical literacy—with the aim of achieving a more socially just society. Our experiences show that these changes in teaching are tied to changes in the ways teachers view children, themselves, and literacy learning. They require teachers to have the courage to face their discursive choices, their logic, and their uncertainties with a sense of agency and responsibility.

GENERALIZABLE TOOLS FOR TRANSFORMATION

In teacher education, the practicum experience is not simply for the experience itself, but for what can be learned from it. The tools we have described are to provide conceptual leverage for transforming that experience into current and future practice. In this book we have offered, not a template, but a series of conceptual and practical tools to help transform learning for teachers, students, professors, and the programs within which they learn. We believe these tools are as applicable to undergraduate and graduate teacher education and special education as they are to the literacy specialists with whom we work, though each group has its special challenges.

We believe the tools are more widely applicable than for our particular students. The success of our new joint program with the Special Education Department, which certifies teachers not only in special education and literacy (birth through sixth grade), but also in elementary teaching, attests to their more general applicability. The fact that one of us (Rogers) has taken the principles to a different university and extended them into an undergraduate and graduate teacher education program further attests to their transportability.

The tools we offer for teacher learning are also applicable to our own learning, as we found with the move to an urban school. We certainly also write our own reflective papers for conferences and for publications such as this. Our own responses to books and articles are a constant feature of our class, as well as our conversations with assistants and among faculty. The ensuing community conversations are always productive. The social justice and critical literacy focus and the discussions surrounding it have forced more clarity for us in our understandings and in our teaching. The celebrations in the lab are an excellent space for our learning, too, as we encounter the array of families and their pride, along with the various discomforts and anxieties of teachers, faculty, and students.

A CONSTANTLY EVOLVING PROGRAM

As we have pointed out, the University at Albany program is structured to ensure the evolution of the Literacy Lab. However, even without that structural impetus toward change, additional tensions actually insist on it. The chafing of our theorizing against the realities of students, teachers, and regularly changing institutional contexts inoculates the course against reification. In the following section, we enumerate some of these less planned factors.

Time

On all levels, time provides constant tensions. We want to accelerate the children's learning, but we also want the children to be in control and to be reflective. We want to establish a parallel framework for the teachers to become reflective while they are engaging in extensive readings, preparing for each tutoring session, and tutoring. Taking time to reflect on our own practice and to work with individual teachers (as they work with individual students), and providing ongoing support for beginning teachers, requires a substantial time commitment. In the meantime, for untenured faculty, the tenure clock is constantly ticking; and in a research university, tenure hinges on publications.

Time is also at a premium for the teachers, who are required by our state regents to obtain a master's degree within 5 years of their beginning teaching—a time at which many are getting married, beginning families, and trying to pay off college loans. This requirement makes it harder to insist on reflective practice. Summer session, squeezed into half the time of a regular semester but taught every day, produces similar tensions but with the compensating advantage of daily continuity.

FINDING EACH TEACHER'S ZPD

As with different kinds of children, different kinds of teachers present different challenges. For example, we encounter teachers who are "naturals"—possessed of many unconsciously productive ways of interacting with children—for whom good teaching is very comfortable. We find some who do not embrace the uncomfortable work of becoming even better teachers, or of becoming critical. We also encounter teachers who view themselves as exemplary and who have been academically very successful, but whose instructional interactions, particularly with minority students, are problematic. Insisting that these teachers confront uncomfortable data from their teaching can be difficult and is often initially accompanied by defensive theorizing. We have shy teachers whom we are asking to be socially forward and make connections with students' families, an undertaking they would normally avoid. There are also those who would avoid family interactions because of cultural discomforts or an unwillingness to confront privilege.

As we work with and learn from our teachers, it is our responsibility to find each teacher's zones of proximal development: the social, intellectual, and emotional spaces in which they are able to make most progress while staying largely in control of their learning. These spaces differ for each teacher in different facets of their pedagogy. Some find reading instruction engaging but struggle to teach writing. For others, word work is their strength and propensity. As instructors, we notice the teachers' strengths, bring these to their attention, and nudge them to bring the strategies that work for them in one area of literacy instruction to other areas. For example, as a teacher notices the ways students construct words, we might ask her to extend this observation and apply it to how texts are constructed. Helping our teachers locate their zone of proximal development, build a physical memory of what it feels like, and figure out how to produce the necessary conditions for it is central for their expansion of what is learned in the lab to the institutional contexts in which they will work.

Name

Over the years we have had different names for the class and space we occupy, beginning with "Clinic." We are mindful of the weight attached to the name of the program, and the differing stakeholders' perspectives on what the name means. Before we moved to Douglass Elementary we shifted the name to the "Literacy Lab" to reflect a less medical model. Currently, this name remains with us at Douglass Elementary. However, for a sixth-grader who must leave his after-school YMCA class to go to a "tutor" in the "Literacy Lab," this name may not have a positive ring. We've considered changing the name to the "University Club," which would potentially reduce this stigma for students. However, "University Club" might lose the legitimacy "Literacy Lab" provides in the school community and the wider sphere of professional organizations. Additionally, any potential name change is associated with tensions around helping meet the school's needs regarding "schooled" literacy. While "Literacy Lab" connotes a wider perspective on literacy practice than "Clinic," it does not yet reflect the integration of critical literacy and an accelerative framework that are at the heart of our practice. Naming our space remains a continuing conversation.

CRITICAL LITERACY/CRITICAL TEACHING

Just as there is no neutral literacy (Dewey, 1985; Kelly, 1995), there is no neutral teaching or teacher education—particularly in literacy. Critical literacy and critical teaching require awareness of the social, historical, and linguistic factors that influence teaching, learning, and literate practice in order to work toward socially just ends. It requires an awareness of privilege and the ability to imagine different possibilities in perspectives and practices. Our development of critical literacy in the class has not been easy. Our stance continues to evolve as we explore critical literacy in theory and practice. This uncertainty has its benefits in openness, but teachers are not always comfortable with it as another open end in their teaching, or as a political responsibility.

Teachers often express an uncertainty about where to focus their attention during their tutoring sessions. They discuss the trade-offs in accelerating students as readers and writers while at the same time developing critical stances toward language and literacy. We find these places of uncertainty (ours and theirs) entry points to highlight the parallel places of learning for students, for teachers, and for teacher educators. Indeed, finding the balance in our teaching is as hard as it is for the teachers taking the Lab course.

A second tension arises from the critical literacy emphasis; consistently confronting privilege and taken-for-granted values can lead teachers to experience critical literacy as a negative stance. Building the positive experience of critical literacy is a constant struggle. A third tension arises between our grounding in the sociocognitive work of Clay (on accelerating children's literate development), and the sociopolitical work on critical literacy (Bomer & Bomer, 2001; Comber & Simpson, 2001; Luke, 2000) and multimodal literacy (Coiro, 2003; Leu & Leu, 2000). Although we have productively integrated Clay's work into the foundations of our critical literacy, struggling with the sociopolitical and multimodal dimensions of literacy can divert attention from struggles with the immediate textual dimensions of print literacy. Similarly, teachers struggling with the discomforts of social values sometimes have less intellectual energy for theorizing about teaching problem-solving on words.

In spite of the tensions, we continue to adhere to the advice of Cochran-Smith (Cochran-Smith, 1995) and Fennimore (Fennimore, 2000), who observes that "successful teacher preparation programs need to be constructed upon commitment to activism as well as to excellence in pedagogical practice" (p. 105).

GROUP VERSUS INDIVIDUAL INSTRUCTION

Over the years, we have struggled with the dilemma of having our teachers work with individual children or with groups. There are advantages and disadvantages to each. Working with individual students makes it possible for the teachers to better understand a student's learning in considerable detail, and to focus on the detail of instructional interactions; working with groups, they often spend more time learning to manage. However, working with groups is more like what the teachers will be routinely required to do. Working with groups may also make critical literacy interactions more productive because of the multiplicity of voices and the built-in disjunctures. However, taking whole groups of children from our colleagues in the after-school program with whom we work could have a disastrous impact on their program. Our current solution is to begin with one-on-one tutoring and, later in the semester, move to collaborative teaching of multiple students for a portion of the instructional time. We continue to look for better solutions, though we are committed to the one-on-one tutorial as a central part of the experience. Our students consistently claim that teaching one-on-one is harder, yet ultimately more intellectually productive, than teaching a whole class.

INSTITUTIONAL NUDGES

Our most recent nudge has come from preparations for accreditation. Following immediately on the heels of reorganizing for changes in state certification structures, the reaccreditation conversations at University at Albany confirmed and streamlined many of our commitments. The practicum course remained a central and intact capstone, now anchoring two programs. One of the new programs, a small joint certification with Special Education, produces cohorts of students. These teachers consistently, and in chorus, use language very differently in their representations of children and in their interactions with them than we have been used to, producing a new kind of challenge.

Most importantly, the accreditation process turned our attention even more to questions of value and evidence. What do we value in preparing literacy teachers? How will these values be made concrete in our practice? How will we know when we have been successful in our efforts? Although we were confident that our course was well organized in just these terms, difficult questions arose around what might count as evidence, and whether some goals should be dropped because of the difficulty of showing evidence that they had been met.

MULTIMODAL LITERACIES

A recent shift in direction is the expansion of children's and teachers' analysis and use of multimodal literacies, and facility with computers—even among first-graders. To restrict the students to print literacy in the tutorial space represents a limited view of literacy (Johnson &

Kress, 2003; Leu & Leu, 2000). However, this produces another tension for us. While we want to help the school successfully meet its obligations to prepare the students for the increased public testing requirements focused on a narrower view of literacy, we also want to extend the children's opportunities and our teachers' thinking. In past semesters, some students have developed PowerPoint presentations for their final celebrations, visited Web sites, written letters to the President to help prevent the destruction of rain forests, and generated reviews for publication on PBS Web sites. These opportunities help the students build identities as writers and researchers, for real purposes and audiences. We are in the process of gaining the expertise and the logic to have students building and critiquing Web sites, but we are not yet there.

COMMUNITY INVOLVEMENT

Over time, we are becoming a part of the school community, with classroom teachers routinely stopping by to talk about their students, to visit the tutoring sessions, and to inquire about the master's program. Parents also stop us in the hallways to request that siblings become involved with the Lab. Nonetheless, we live in fear to some degree that the principal, Bob White, will retire before we become a fully integrated part of the institution. Because of our lack of fiscal or structural embeddedness in the school, we must rely on the goodwill of administrators, teachers, staff, and parents. Fortunately, this has become increasingly likely as the school hires more of our graduates. Additionally, one of us been asked to engage with the teachers for several long-term professional development initiatives.

In recent semesters, our first-seminar sessions have been visits to the Community Health Center across the street from the school and to a local church to learn from and talk with community leaders. These experiences beyond the school walls have opened new possibilities for engaging with and learning from the community.

LEADERSHIP

There are inherent tensions in expecting our teachers to take up leadership in matters of literacy teaching and policy. We expect our teachers to actively problem-solve; to articulate their pedagogical knowledge, skills, and competencies; to act with authority while keeping open the possibility of alternative practices and perspectives; and to question the very foundations from which they act. In other words, we simultaneously expect from them more authority and less certainty, particularly as they explore their own, and each other's, practice. We view leadership as a question of human resource development, and our intention is for teachers to lead by developing communities of practice committed to action research. Of course, building such communities in the context of powerful state and federal efforts that oppose self-determination at the local level is problematic, to say the least. Even teachers' certification as "literacy specialists" works against building horizontal rather than hierarchical communities of practice. In such constrained and hierarchical contexts it is hard enough to even ask questions about the nature and development of practice. Asking such questions in ways that also examine their values and commitments, and the significance of their practice for their own and their students' lives, is particularly difficult (McNiff & Whitehead, 2000).

CONCLUSION

In the reflective essays teachers write at the end of the class, and in conversations, they report a tension between the satisfaction (indeed, relief) in completing their master's program, and the realization that they will soon face fewer opportunities for collaborative intellectual challenge. Confronting their learning histories and trajectories as professionals and public intellectuals, they view themselves as different people with a responsibility, but also a need for ongoing intellectual stimulation.

This book has served some of these functions for us, but it does not offer, nor do we seek, closure. Working through the tensions we have described in this chapter will certainly lead us to new experiments and possibilities. The process will also lead us to a better understanding of our own teaching as we continue through the cycles of planning, acting, documenting, and reflecting (Carr & Kemmis, 1986). However, there is no doubt that writing this book to broaden our audience has been an excellent tool for developing our own practice. In the 3 years we have tinkered with the book, the disjunctures we encountered as we committed to print, as we reviewed one another's work, and as we negotiated the writing while continuing to teach have changed the ways we teach, and changed us. The book has been a critical part of our action research, as others have also found (Atweh,

Kemmis, & Weeks, 1998; McKernan, 1991). It has not only made our teaching-learning-research more consciously about community knowledge production and stewardship, but it has consistently energized our efforts. At the same time, it has driven home the fact that "learning to teach . . . is the work of a lifetime" (Cook-Sather, 2001, p. 36), whether teaching children or teaching teachers.

Afterword:
Two Perspectives

"IT'S A WIN-WIN"—ROBERT WHITE, PRINCIPAL

Robert White, an African American, is the principal of the school. His roots in the school district are 33 years deep. He began as a middle school and high school science teacher and has been principal of the school for 5 years. In 2003, Mr. White was recognized as Public Citizen of the Year by a local community group. He was nominated for the award by three of his staff members in part because of his strong commitment to, and involvement with, families and the school community. This afterword offers his perspective on how the Literacy Lab fits into his plans.

I enjoy working at Douglass Elementary. The students are terrific and I am committed to their care and education. Arbor Hill is an inner-city school, and we have to face issues that impact the education of our children that schools in more privileged districts do not. As principal, I find there are many people offering some form of help. My job is to select programs that are consistent with the intentions and needs of the school. I do not want programs pulling us in many different directions.

The University at Albany program is an excellent after-school program because it's a win-win for Albany and for our school. We get graduate-level students who have the chance to tutor one-on-one, and their students have the opportunity to work with our students in our school. Our students are tutored at the end of the school day and are not pulled from their regular classrooms, as happens with some of our academic intervention services. I also like the fact that I can draw from candidates in the program when I hire new teachers. These prospective teachers have already been in the building and know the students they will be teaching and their families.

During the SUNY program, as I watch the final presentations, I

175

see the high level of family involvement. Families like to come out for presentations, and this is a chance for them to celebrate what their children have learned in the program. I have seen the students grow over the time the program has been here. Earlier, the children were more tentative during the presentations. Now, they are more confident.

It is important to me that I am at Arbor Hill. Through my assistance to my staff, I start children, most who now live in poverty, on the first leg of their journey toward becoming productive, successful adults. My goal is to have all of our children break the cycle of poverty through the benefits that they will receive from acquiring a good education. The program at the University at Albany helps me work toward that goal.

"GRANDMA, YOU GOT TIME? PAPA, YOU GOT TIME? I WANT TO READ TO YOU": RETHA BROWN, GRANDMOTHER

This afterword focuses on one grandmother's experience with her grandson's involvement in the Literacy Lab. Retha Brown discusses the changes she has noticed in her grandson Marcus's development as a reader and writer, her experiences of (and preferences for) interactions with each teacher, and the ways she supports Marcus as a reader and writer at home.

I think this lab has been a great asset to Marcus. When Marcus started day care, we knew that he had problems and they were working with him then. When he came to Douglass Elementary, I knew that he was going to be behind. But with this reading program, I think it's helped get him up to par. I've seen a lot of progress. When he started he couldn't read books. I've seen where before he would actually skip over small words. He wouldn't take the time to figure them out. Now, he does not skip over anything, he tries to pronounce it. The biggest change I saw was when he was able to read the commercial. I'm still impressed with that. A commercial came on TV that had some words to it and he just stood there and just read it right out, no problem. I couldn't believe it. It was the first time I saw him actually go to the TV and read something back and he did it so clearly.

Marcus takes his time when he reads now. He really tries. He gives it a good effort. He prefers to take his time to try to read something, rather than having me tell him. He'll try and try and try to sound that word out and he doesn't give up anymore. He wants to read everything about sports now. His tutor gave him a basketball and a book about Michael Jordan. He was very excited. At the end of the time he was reading chapter books. He said, "Grandma, Grandma, I can read chapter books now." He was very proud of himself. I told him he had every right to be proud of himself. This program is a great asset.

In this program, you guys spend a lot of time with these kids. You give them individual attention and I'm sure you have a lot of patience. When he brings home the books, I try to reinforce what they've been doing that day. I keep him on top of it so he doesn't forget things. He gets something to read every night. Since going to this program, reading has become easier for him. He looks forward to doing his homework and he walks around the house, "Grandma, you got time? Papa, you got time? I want to read to you." He's looking for someone to read to every night. At home he reads Dr. Seuss and basketball books. He's really into the basketball thing, sports books, even magazines. I pick up *Highlights* magazine. I love those and figure they would help him.

I think what the last tutor teaches the next one comes right in and picks it up. They build upon what happened the time before and you're doing it in a good fashion. I'm really impressed with it. We are always moving forward with this program. It's not like he's stuck and we have to get ready to start all over. Each tutor builds on the semester before. Marcus has enjoyed this program from the start, from the very beginning. All the tutors have seemed to care. They have genuine care about these kids. It's not that they're just here because they have to be. His tutors still stay in touch. They've written letters to him after they finished.

The tutors have communicated with my family in many ways. I liked the e-mails the best. I've also used journals and family stories where I put stories on a tape recorder. The tutors got to know a lot about Marcus with the pictures they took and the pictures we sent in. That gave an opportunity to find out the things that he liked. They put the pictures in albums. I think I've taught the tutors that I'm supportive, that parents can be right there with their children every step of the way. We worked together. My husband told the tutors that he wanted Marcus not just to pronounce the words; that he had to understand the words when he read.

When I tell other parents about the lab, I tell them it's a reading lab where teachers give the children additional help to bring them up to par to make sure they're on their grade level. It's an excellent program. In addition to becoming better readers, it may help with other fears the children have, like with presentations. Most kids are afraid to talk in front of people. So they're getting other things out of it other than just reading. As a parent, you reinforce and help at home what they're learning here. We work along with you guys. It's a team thing. I send my child to school to enhance what he has learned at home. You teach your children at home. And you guys are really great with enhancing that. That's the biggest thing, a team. It's all about team-work. At the end of the semester, you send home a refrigerator sheet with ideas. They're great. If he does forget some things, he'll always go back and look at them. He gets different ideas each time. I wish you met more with the children; two times a week isn't enough.

I grew up near Douglass Elementary. So I'm familiar with the school. I heard a lot of negative things about Douglass Elementary before I put him here. A lot. I decided to take my chances. After I got him here, after the first meeting, when I heard Mr. White speak, I knew then this was the right school. I could truly see the care and concern that would come from the staff. And I know we're not going to have a child just pushed along. The statistics, whatever that may be, fine. I see that these people here are truly involved, and they truly show care, a care and concern for these kids. I really like Douglass Elementary.

Appendix:
Evolutionary Context

The evolution of our practice has been affected by the range of instructors and teachers, and by the historical and institutional context. As with other teacher education programs, the faculty teaching the practica have almost all been female and untenured, with some adjunct faculty. The only faculty member to get tenure whose consistent responsibility was teaching the practicum course, to date, is male. The extra teaching load associated with the course has been born by faculty with little or no recognition from the university. While the course was a 6-credit course for the teachers taking it, because of the contact time, for faculty it counted as one 3-credit teaching load. Two years ago this discrepancy was rectified. The class was nomadic for many years, managing space wherever it could be found. For another 16 years we were located in the old teacher's college building, which allowed us to have one-way viewing areas, upon which we relied heavily. Our current location in a high-poverty, urban, largely minority elementary school was planned for a number of reasons. First, although we had previously been located in the downtown area, for a number of reasons our clientele had largely been suburban mainstream students (albeit, often marginalized in special education). We became increasingly aware that we could act in a more socially just manner by serving the greater need among local urban minority students. Second, the fact that our teachers had virtually no experience working with children with different cultural backgrounds meant that it was necessary for them to acquire such experience.

CURRICULAR CONTEXT

The class is the final practicum experience in our main master's program, which provides teachers with the master's degree plus certification as Literacy Specialists Birth through sixth grade. For the instructional and certification context of the practicum class, see the department Web site at www.albany.edu/reading. The Web site provides details of program structure and individual class structure, along with proposed assignments and course readings. To obtain a current syllabus for the course, go to the department Web site.

STRUCTURE OF THE COURSE

Class meets twice a week during regular semesters and five times a week during summer sessions. We would prefer daily meetings during the regular semester to have more continuity and to be more effective in teaching the students, but there are major structural obstacles in accomplishing this. There are also trade-offs. The summer session has daily meetings, but insufficient time for teacher reflection, and a disarticulation between the teachers' classroom teaching and their practicum teaching.

During the first hour of each session the teachers teach a student and are videotaped or observed by the instructor, co-instructor, or other teachers whose students may be absent that day. When the students are returned to their after-school classrooms, the teachers are provided with a half-hour debriefing period in which they engage in a collaborative or prompted reflection (see tools 8 and 13). After the debriefing period, there is a seminar that revolves around a set of class readings and a videotaped teaching session (see tools 9 and 15).

In outline form, the structure is:

4:00–5:00   teaching
5:00–5:30   debriefing or structured reflection
5:30–6:15   seminar around videotaped session
6:15–7:00   seminar around class readings

The teaching sessions are initially one-to-one and are structured essentially as Clay (1993) suggests, with variation that results from age/performance differences, and the 1-hour rather than 30-minute instructional frame. Writing is accorded similar time to reading, but also depends on the point of development. Analysis and synthesis of words takes about 10 minutes during the hour.

TEACHERS

As with most teacher education programs in the country, our Literacy Specialist preparation program is populated primarily by middle-class white women, with occasional minorities (2%, none of whom are male) and men (9%). These teachers (most of whom remain classroom teachers) are generally either already teaching, or are going to graduate school full-time between completing their undergraduate teacher preparation program and taking up a full-time position. We also have a small group of women returning to the workforce after raising a family. Most of our teachers attend because in New York State teachers are required to obtain a master's degree within 5 years of their initial teaching. Since we have both part-time and full-time students, it is not possible to have a cohort system, but we try to build a sense of community along the way.

STUDENTS

Until the summer of 2000, our students were referrals from a wide range of sources: school psychologists, teachers, administrators, reading teachers, and parents. We also had occasional self-referrals from adults. In the summer of 2000 we moved into the high-poverty, inner-city K-6 elementary school whose population is 98% minority. This change in student population along with the change in venue had a powerful impact on the program. It complicated our lives substantially in terms of scheduling, coordination with after-school and summer programs, and regularity of attendance, but at the same time it brought indispensable advantages to all parties.

OURSELVES

We, too, are white and middle-class. Each of us has had experience at the elementary school level as classroom teachers and/or reading teachers. Each of us has experience working in inner-city schools in some capacity. Two of us (Cheryl and Peter) have children (three each), a factor that we do not think irrelevant given that our class is taught in the evenings, routinely obliterating home mealtimes twice a week (thrice until recently).

Each course is taught with a teaching assistant who is either a doctoral student or a strong graduate of our master's program interested in continuing studies and possibly moving into the doctoral program.

RELATIONSHIPS, FEEDBACK, AND GRADES

Teachers entering our program have high undergraduate grade point averages. They expect to continue to earn high grades, and are often anxious about their grade as the semester progresses, dragging their attention away from reflective practice. We respond to all of their written work. However, we view initial assessments, instructional logs, reflective journals, and written updates as works in progress, and do not assign grades to their early assignments. This is difficult for some. As one student put it, "Cheryl, it's twenty years of schooling moving us this way [to look for a grade]."

There is an important element of trust involved in this arrangement, because the teachers will be graded at the end of the semester. New aspects of their instruction will be drawn to their attention throughout the semester, not only by instructors, but also by colleagues and students. Some end up with a less than perfect grade despite having had generally supportive, constructive feedback throughout. Serious problems are addressed when they arise, and sometimes sessions are devoted to confronting these head-on.

Grading is a constant tension for us and for the teachers, since the grading serves a certification function. However, teachers are not working in equal situations, not only because some have classrooms of their own to learn from, but also because there are very real differences between the students assigned to different teachers.

The tension around grading is part of wider tensions around power and control. The state Regents' requirement of a master's degree within 5 years of initial certification—followed by a state test in the specialization area chosen—has forced many teachers to regard their professional development as jumping through another hoop. The time constraints mean that anything seen as nonessential to that goal is not viewed favorably. Grading reinforces that power-identity structure both in the teachers and in their instructors.

We do not deny our institutional power, which is evident in the grade, and use it to insist that teachers invest energies in particular areas and thereby shift their interests and goals. This puts us in the same kind of struggle as the teachers in trying to arrange for children to take control of their own learning.

The power differential in grading also creates an additional problem for us in terms of monitoring our own practice. For example, reflective writing is one source of evidence we use. However, this source can be compromised by what the writer thinks the instructor wants to hear. Fortunately, this tendency is limited by our requirement of specific examples, and it is balanced by the range of sources of evidence available.

INSTITUTIONAL ORGANIZATION AND COOPERATION

While operating at the university we operated under a "noblesse oblige" arrangement, provided there was no trouble. Trouble occasionally occurred with impatient parents calling the university president. We constantly had to defend our space from those with more resources.

The initial move to the school site brought new problems. We needed to develop relationships with the staff; secure sites for materials, seminars, and the tutorials; and now operate within the school district calendar, rather than the university calendar. After gaining approval from the assistant superintendent to establish the Literacy Lab at Douglass Elementary, several meetings were held—with the principal, assistant principal, YMCA coordinator, and summer school teacher coordinator—in which we specified our needs and what we felt we could offer. During these meetings, the details of the program were discussed. It was decided that students selected for our program would include students already enrolled in the school summer program. This helped initially to secure students. With the support of the YMCA coordinator, we established locations for the seminar sessions, tutoring, and supplies (leveled books, materials, video equipment). These locations have required adjustments along the way. Since we normally hold class in the faculty meeting room, when other school or district meetings take place in that room, we move to the art room where the art teacher has generously allowed us space. Our locked storage closet is less than we had hoped for and currently being renegotiated. The books are crammed into it and we have so far lost five video cameras from it, four in one semester and one subsequently.

During fall 2000, the first time the Lab was held at the school during a school year, several issues needed to be addressed anew. Teachers enrolled in the fall and spring semesters also followed the city school district calendar (including superintendents' conference days, field trips, and holidays) rather than the university calendar. Issues related to student attendance took a great deal of time during the fall semester, and continue to do so. Initially, we tried to include students who were not enrolled in the after-school program, but who had attended the summer program. However, they rarely attended the sessions, and attendance is critical not only for them, but for the teachers in the program. Now we include only students in the after-school program and with a history of good attendance.

During the second year, as we began to better understand the ethos and intricacies of the school, we worked collaboratively with the school's two reading teachers, excellent graduates of our program, to select students to tutor. As we become more established in the school, our relationships with the teachers in the building, with the administration, and with the families of the students become more secure. Now, 4 years in, the classroom teachers stop by to talk to the tutors and share insights about the students enrolled in the program. We are beginning to attract graduate students from among the school's teachers. The arrangement is mutually beneficial, as we hope the two cases in the afterword suggest.

References

Allen, J., Fabregas, V., Hankins, K., Hull, G., Labbo, L., Lawson, H., et al. (2002). PhOLKS lore: Learning from photographs, families, and children. *Language arts, 79*(4), 312–322.

Allington, R. L. (1994). What's special about special programs for children who find learning to read difficult? *Journal of Reading Behavior, 26*, 1–21.

Alvermann, D. E., & Xu, S. H. (2003). Children's everyday literacies: Intersections of popular culture and langauge arts instruction. *Language Arts, 81*(2), 145–154.

Anders, P. L., Hoffman, J. V., & Duffy, G. G. (2000). Teaching teachers to teach reading: Paradigm shifts, persistent problems, and challenges. In M. L. Kamil, P. B. Mosenthal, P. D. Pearson, & R. Barr (Eds.), *Handbook of reading research* (Vol. 3, pp. 719–742). Mahwah, NJ: Erlbaum.

Anderson, C. (2000). *How's it going?: A practical guide to conferring with student writers.* Portsmouth, NH: Heinemann.

Atweh, B., Kemmis, S., & Weeks, P. (Eds.). (1998). *Action research in practice: Partnerships for social justice in education.* London: Routledge.

Banks, J. A. (Ed.). (2003). *Diversity and citizenship education: Global perspectives.* San Francisco: Jossey-Bass.

Banks, J. A., & Banks, C. (1995). Equity pedagogy: An essential component of multicultural education. *Theory into Practice, 34*(3), 152–158.

Bear, D., Invernizzi, M., & Johnston, F. (2003). *Words their way: Word study for phonics, vocabulary & spelling instruction* (3rd ed.). Upper Saddle River, NJ: Merrill/Prentice-Hall.

Beyer, L. E. (Ed.). (1996). *Creating democratic classrooms: The struggle to integrate theory and practice.* New York: Teachers College Press.

Bigelow, B., Christensen, L., Karp, S., Miner, B., & Peterson, B. (Eds.). (1994). *Rethinking our classrooms: Teaching for justice* (Vol. 1). Milwaukee, WI: Rethinking Schools.

Bigelow, B., Christensen, L., Karp, S., Miner, B., & Peterson, B. (Eds.). (2001). *Rethinking our classrooms: Teaching for justice* (Vol. 2). Milwaukee, WI: Rethinking Schools.

Bomer, R., & Bomer, K. (2001). *For a better world: Reading and writing for social action.* Portsmouth, NH: Heinemann.

Brandts, L. (1999). Are pullout programs sabotaging classroom community in our elementary schools? *Primary Voices, 7*(3), 9–15.

Braus, N., & Geidel, M. (2000). *Everyone's kids' books: A guide to multicultural, socially conscious books for children.* Brattelboro, VT: Everyone's Kids Books.

Bruner, J. (1987). Life as narrative. *Social Research, 54*(1), 11–32.

Cagan, E. (1978, May). Individualism, collectivism, and radical educational reform. *Harvard Educational Review, 48,* 228.

Cambourne, B. (1995). Toward an educationally relevant theory of literacy learning: Twenty years of inquiry. *The Reading Teacher, 49*(3), 182–190.

Cambourne, B. (2002). The conditions of learning: Is learning natural? *The Reading Teacher, 55*(8), 758–762.

Carr, W., & Kemmis, S. (1986). *Becoming critical: Knowing through action research.* London: Falmer Press.

Clay, M. M. (1987). Learning to be learning disabled. *New Zealand Journal of Educational Studies, 22,* 155–173.

Clay, M. M. (1991a). *Becoming literate: The construction of inner control.* Portsmouth, NH: Heinemann.

Clay, M. M. (1991b). Introducing a new storybook to young readers. *The Reading Teacher, 45*(4), 264–272.

Clay, M. M. (1993a). *An observation survey of early literacy achievement.* Portsmouth, NH: Heinemann.

Clay, M. M. (1993b). *Reading Recovery: A guidebook for teachers in training.* Portsmouth, NH: Heinemann.

Clay, M. M. (1998). *By different paths to common outcomes.* York, ME: Stenhouse.

Clay, M. M. (2001). *Change over time in children's literacy development.* Portsmouth, NH: Heinemann.

Cochran-Smith, M. (1995). Uncertain allies: Understanding the boundaries of race and teaching. *Harvard Educational Review, 65*(4), 541–570.

Cochran-Smith, M. (2000). Blind vision: Unlearning racism in teacher education. *Harvard Educational Review, 70*(2), 157–190.

Cochran-Smith, M., & Lytle, S. L. (2001). Beyond certainty: Taking an inquiry stance on practice. In A. Lieberman & L. Miller (Eds.), *Teachers caught in the action: Professional development that matters* (pp. 45–58). New York: Teachers College Press.

Cochran-Smith, M., & Lytle, S. L. (1993). *Inside/outside: Teacher research and knowledge.* New York: Teachers College Press.

Coiro, J. (2003). Exploring literacy on the internet: Reading comprehension on the internet: Expanding our understanding of reading comprehension to encompass new literacies. *Reading Teacher, 56*(5), 458–464.

Cole, A., & Knowles, J. G. (2000). *Researching teaching: Exploring teacher development through reflective inquiry.* Boston, MA: Allyn and Bacon.

Collins, J., & Blot, R. K. (2003). *Literacy and literacies: Texts, power, and identity.* New York: Cambridge University Press.

Collins, P. (1998). *Fighting words: Black women and the search for justice.* Minneapolis: University of Minnesota Press.

Comber, B., & Simpson, A. (Eds.). (2001). *Negotiating critical literacies in classrooms.* Mahwah, NJ: Erlbaum.

Comber, B., Thompson, P., & Wells, M. (2001). Critical literacy finds a "place":

Writing and social action in low-income Australian grade 2/3 classrooms. *The Elementary School Journal, 101*(4), 451–464.

Commeyras, M. (1994). Were Janell and Nessie in the same classroom? Questions as the first order of reality in storybook discussions. *Language Arts, 71*, 517–523.

Compton-Lilly, C. (2003). *Reading families: The literate lives of urban children.* New York: Teachers College Press.

Cook-Gumperz, J. (1986). *The social construction of literacy.* Cambridge: Cambridge University Press.

Cook-Sather, A. (2001). Translating themselves: Becoming a teacher through text and talk. In C. M. Clark (Ed.), *Talking shop: Authentic conversation and teacher learning* (pp. 16–39). New York: Teachers College Press.

Cope, B., & Kalantzus, M. (Eds.). (1993). *The powers of literacy: A genre approach to teaching writing.* Pittsburgh, PA: University of Pittsburgh Press.

Cunningham, P. M. (1999). *Phonics they use: Words for reading and writing* (3rd ed.). Reading, MA: Addison-Wesley.

Darling-Hammond, L., & McLaughlin, M. W. (1999). Investing in teaching as a learning profession: Policy problems and prospects. In L. Darling-Hammond & G. Sykes (Eds.), *Teaching as the learning profession: Handbook of policy and practice* (pp. 376–411). San Francisco: Jossey-Bass.

Denos, C. H. (2003). Negotiating for positions of power in primary classrooms. *Language Arts, 80*(6), 416–424.

Derry, S. J., & Potts, M. K. (1998). How tutors model students: A study of personal constructs in adaptive tutoring. *American Educational Research Journal, 35*(1), 65–99.

Dewey, J. (1985). *Democracy and education.* Carbondale, IL: Southern Illinois University Press.

Dozier, C. (2001). *Constructing teacher knowledge: Learning from the field.* Unpublished doctoral dissertation, University at Albany, State University of New York.

Dozier, C., Johnston, P. H., & Delsanto, D. (2001). *A fine-grained analysis of struggling middle school readers and productive instruction.* Paper presented at the International Reading Association, New Orleans, LA.

Dozier, C., & Rutten, I. (in press). Responsive teaching toward responsive teachers: Mediating transfer through intentionality, enactment, and articulation. *Journal of Literacy Research.*

Edwards, P. (1999). *A path to follow.* Portsmouth, NH: Heinemann.

Elbers, E., & Streefland, L. (2000). "Shall we be researchers again?" Identity and social interaction in a community of inquiry. In H. Cowie & G. V. D. Aalsvoort (Eds.), *Social interaction in learning and instruction: The meaning of discourse for the construction of knowledge* (pp. 35–51). Amsterdam: Pergamon Press.

Fairclough, N. (1992). *Discourse and social change.* London: Longman.

Fecho, B. (2000). Critical inquiries into language in an urban classroom. *Research in the Teaching of English, 34*(3), 368–395.

Fecho, B., & Allen, J. (2002). Teachers researching communities of practice for social justice. *The School Field, 12*(3/4), 117–140.

Fennimore, B. S. (2000). *Talk matters: Refocusing the language of public school.* New York: Teachers College Press.

Fishman, S. M., & McCarthy, L. (2000). *Unplayed tapes: A personal history of collaborative teacher research.* New York: Teachers College Press/National Council of Teachers of English.

Fletcher, R. (1996). *A writer's notebook: Unlocking the writer within you.* New York: Avon Camelot.

Fletcher, R. (2002). *Poetry matters: Writing a poem from the Inside Out.* New York: Harper Trophy.

Fountas, I. C., & Pinnell, G. S. (1996). *Guided reading: Good first teaching for all children.* Portsmouth, NH: Heinemann.

Fountas, I. C., & Pinnell, G. S. (1999). *Matching books to readers: Using leveled books in guided reading, K–3.* Portsmouth, NH: Heinemann.

Freire, P., & Macedo, D. (1987). *Literacy: Reading the word and the world.* Hadley, MA: Bergin and Garvey.

Freppon, P. (2001). *What it takes to be a teacher: The role of personal and professional development.* Portsmouth, NH: Heinemann.

Gee, J. P. (1996). *Social linguistics and literacies: Ideology in discourses* (2nd ed.). London: Taylor & Francis.

Gee, J. P. (1997). Thinking, learning, and reading: The situated sociocultural mind. In D. Kirshner & J. A. Whitson (Eds.), *Situated cognition: Social, semiotic, and psychological perspectives* (pp. 37–55). Mahwah, NJ: Erlbaum.

Gioia, B. (2001). The emergent language and literacy experiences of three deaf preschoolers. *International Journal of Disability, Development & Education* (Vol. 48, pp. 411–428).

Gioia, B., & Johnston, P. H. (1998). The university reading club. In D. H. Evensen & P. B. Mosenthal (Eds.), *Reconsidering the role of the reading clinic in a new age of literacy* (Vol. 6, pp. 177–196). Stamford, CT: JAI Press.

Giroux, H. A. (1983). *Theory and resistance in education: a pedagogy for the opposition.* South Hadley, MA: Bergin & Garvey.

Glasswell, K., Parr, J. M., & McNaughton, S. (2003). Working with William: Teaching, learning, and the joint construction of a struggling writer. *Reading Teacher, 56*(5), 494–500.

Goldstein, L. S. (1999). The relational zone: The role of caring relationships in the co-construction of mind. *American Educational Research Journal, 36*(3), 647–673.

Goodman, Y. (1978). Kidwatching: Observing children in the classroom. In A. Jagger & M. T. Smith-Burke (Eds.), *Observing the language learner* (pp. 9–18). Newark, DE: International Reading Association.

Graves, D. H. (1989). *Investigate nonfiction.* Portsmouth, NH: Heinemann.

Grossen, M. (2000). Institutional framings in thinking, learning and teaching. In H. Cowie & G. V. D. Aalsvoort (Eds.), *Social interaction in learning and instruction: The meaning of discourse for the construction of knowledge* (pp. 21–34). Amsterdam: Pergamon Press.

Harre, R., & Gillet, G. (1994). *The discursive mind.* Thousand Oaks, CA: Sage.

Harvey, S. (1998). *Nonfiction matters.* York, ME: Stenhouse.

Heath, S. B. (1983). *Ways with words.* Cambridge, MA: Cambridge University Press.

Heshusius, L. (1995). Listening to children: "What could we possibly have in common?" From concerns with self to participatory consciousness. *Theory into Practice, 34*(2), 117–123.

Hoffman, J., & Pearson, P. D. (2000). Reading teacher education in the next millenium: What your grandmother's teacher didn't know that your granddaughter's teacher should. *Reading Research Quarterly, 35*(1), 28–44.

Holdaway, D. (1979). *The foundations of literacy.* Gosford, Australia: Ashton-Scholastic.

Holland, D., & Quinn, N. (1987). *Cultural models in language and thought.* Cambridge, England: Cambridge University Press.

hooks, b. (1994). *Teaching to transgress.* New York: Routledge.

Hume, K. (2001). Seeing shades of gray: Developing knowledge-building community through science. In G. Wells (Ed.), *Action talk and text: Learning and teaching through inquiry* (pp. 99–117). New York: Teachers College Press.

Hymes, D. (1991). Ethnopoetics and sociolinguistics: Three stories by African-American children. In I. G. Maclom (Ed.), *Linguistics in the service of society* (pp. 155–170). Perth, Australia: Institute of Applied Linguistics, Edith Cowman University.

Johnson, D., & Kress, G. (2003). Globalisation, literacy and society: Redesigning pedagogy and assessment. *Assessment in Education, 10*(1), 5–14.

Johnston, P. H. (1985). Understanding reading failure: A case study approach. *Harvard Educational Review, 55,* 153–177.

Johnston, P. H. (1989). Constructive evaluation and the improvement of teaching and learning. *Teachers College Record, 90*(4), 509–528.

Johnston, P. H. (1992). *Constructive evaluation of literate activity.* White Plains, NY: Longman.

Johnston, P. H. (1997). *Knowing literacy: Constructive literacy assessment.* York, ME: Stenhouse.

Johnston, P. H. (2004). *Choice words: How our language affects children's learning.* York, ME: Stenhouse.

Johnston, P. H., & Backer, J. (2002). Inquiry and a good conversation: "I learn a lot from them." In R. L. Allington & P. H. Johnston (Eds.), *Reading to learn: Lessons from exemplary fourth-grade classrooms* (pp. 37–53). New York: Guilford.

Johnston, P. H., Bennett, T., & Cronin, J. (2002). "I want students who are thinkers." In R. L. Allington & P. H. Johnston (Eds.), *Reading to learn: Lessons from exemplary fourth-grade classrooms* (pp. 140–165). New York: Guilford.

Johnston, P. H., Dozier, C., & Grand, J. (2000, November). *Reflective inquiry: Building productive instruction for struggling middle school students.* Paper presented at the National Reading Conference.

Johnston, P. H., & Quinlan, M. E. (2002). A caring, responsible learning community. In R. L. Allington & P. H. Johnston (Eds.), *Reading to learn: Lessons from exemplary fourth-grade classrooms* (pp. 123–139). New York: Guilford.

Juel, C. (1996). What makes literacy tutoring effective? *Reading Research Quarterly, 31*(3), 268–289.

Kamberelis, G. (1999). Genre development and learning: Children writing stories, science reports and poems. *Research in the Teaching of English, 43,* 403–460.

Kelly, E. E. (1995). *Education, democracy, and public knowledge.* San Francisco, CA: Westview Press.

Kemmis, S., & Wilkinson, M. (1998). Participatory action research and the study of practice. In B. Atweh, S. Kemmis, & P. Weeks (Eds.), *Action research in practice: Partnerships for social justice in education* (pp. 21–36). New York: Routledge.

Kerr, D. H. (1996). Democracy, nurturance, and community. In R. Soder (Ed.), *Democracy, education, and the schools* (pp. 37–68). San Francisco: Jossey-Bass.

Knoblauch, C., & Brannon, L. (1988). Knowing our knowledge: A phenomenological basis for teacher research. In L. Z. Smith (Ed.), *Audits of meaning: A festschrift in honor of Ann E. Berthoff.* Portsmouth, NH: Heinemann/Boynton/Cook.

Knoblauch, C., & Brannon, L. (1993). *Critical teaching and the idea of literacy.* Portsmouth, NH: Boynton/Cook.

Kos, R. (1991). Persistence of reading disabilities: The voices of four middle school students. *American Educational Research Journal, 28,* 875–895.

Kyle, D. W., McIntyre, E., Miller, K., & Moore, G. (2002). *Reaching out: A K–8 resource for connecting with families.* Thousand Oaks, CA: Corwin Press.

Ladson-Billings, G. (1994). *The dreamkeepers: Successful teachers of African American children.* San Francisco: Jossey-Bass.

Lave, J. (1996). Teaching, as learning, in practice. *Mind, Culture, and Activity, 3*(3), 149–164.

Leu, D. J. Jr., & Leu, D. D. (2000). *Teaching with the internet: Lessons from the classroom* (3rd ed.). Norwood, MA: Christopher-Gordon.

Lewis, C., Ketter, J., & Fabos, B. (2001). Reading race in a rural context. *International journal of qualitative studies in education, 14*(3), 317–350.

Lewison, M., Flint, A. S., & Sluys, K. V. (2002). Taking on critical literacy: The journey of newcomers. *Language Arts, 79*(5), 382–392.

Litowitz, B. E. (1993). Deconstruction in the zone of proximal development. In E. A. Forman, N. Minick, & C. A. Stone (Eds.), *Contexts for learning: Sociocultural dynamics in children's development* (pp. 184–196). New York: Oxford University Press.

Luke, A. (2000). Critical literacy in Australia: A matter of context and standpoint. *Journal of Adolescent and Adult Literacy, 43*(5), 448–461.

Luke, A. (2004). Notes on the future of critical discourse studies. *Critical Discourse Studies, 1*(1), 149–152.

Luke, C., & Gore, J. (Eds). (1992). *Feminisms and critical pedagogy*. New York: Routledge.

Lyons, C. A., Pinnell, G. S., & DeFord, D. E. (1993). *Partners in learning: Teachers and children in Reading Recovery*. New York: Teachers College Press.

Lytle, S. L. (2000). Teacher research in the contact zone. In M. L. Kamil, P. B. Mosenthal, P. D. Pearson, & R. Barr (Eds.), *Handbook of reading research* (Vol. 3, pp. 691–718). Mahwah, NJ: Erlbaum.

McKernan, J. (1991). *Curriculum action research: A handbook of methods and resources for the reflective practitioner*. London: Kegan Page.

McNiff, J., & Whitehead, J. (2000). *Action research in organizations*. London: Routledge.

Mercer, N. (2000). *Words and minds: How we use language to think together*. London: Routledge.

Merseth, K. K. (1996). Cases and case methods in teacher education. In T. B. J. Sikula & E. Guyton (Ed.), *Handbook of research on teacher education* (pp. 722–744). New York: Macmillan.

Moje, E. B. (1997). Exploring discourse, subjectivity, and knowledge in chemistry class. *Journal of Classroom Interaction, 32*(2), 35–44.

Moll, L. C., Amanti, C., Neff, D., & Gonzalez, N. (1992). Funds of knowledge for teaching: Using a qualitative approach to connect homes and classrooms. *Theory into Practice, 31,* 132–141.

Moll, L. C., Saez, R., & Dworin, J. (2001). Exploring biliteracy: Two student case examples of writing as social practice. *The Elementary School Journal, 101*(4), 435–449.

National Commission on Teaching and America's Future. (1996). *What matters most: Teaching for America's future*. New York: National Commission on Teaching and America's Future.

New London Group. (1996). A pedagogy of multiliteracies: Designing social futures. *Harvard Educational Review, 66*(1), 60–92.

Nicholls, J. G. (1989). *The competitive ethos and democratic education*. Cambridge, MA: Harvard University Press.

Nieto, S. (2000). *Affirming diversity: The sociopolitical context of multicultural education* (3rd ed.). New York: Longman.

Noddings, N. (1992). *The challenge to care in schools: An alternative approach to education*. New York: Teachers College Press.

Noffke, S. E. (1995). Action research and democratic schooling: Problematics and potentials. In S. E. Noffke & R. B. Stevenson (Eds.), *Educational action research: Becoming practically critical* (pp. 1–10). New York: Teachers College Press.

O'Brien, J. (2001). Children reading critically: A local history. In B. Comber & A. Simpson (Eds.), *Negotiating critical literacies in classrooms* (pp. 37–54). Mahwah, NJ: Erlbaum.

Ogle, D. (1986). K-W-L: A teaching model that develops active reading of expository text. *The Reading Teacher, 39,* 564–570.

Ohlhausen, M., & Jepsen, M. (1992). Lessons from Goldilocks: Somebody's been choosing my books but I can make my own choices now! *The New Advocate, 5*(1), 31–47.

Orellana, M. F., & Hernandez, A. (1999). Talking the walk: Children reading urban environmental print. *The Reading Teacher, 52*(6), 612–619.

Peck, S. M. (2000). *Now we know something: Elementary teachers' perspectives on change in reading instruction.* Unpublished doctoral dissertation, University at Albany, State University of New York.

Perfect, K. A. (1999). Rhyme and reason: Poetry for the heart and head. *The Reading Teacher, 52,* 228–232.

Peyton-Young, J. (2001). Displaying practices of masculinity: Critical literacy and social contexts. *Journal of Adolescent and Adult Literacy, 45*(1), 4–14.

Pinnell, G. S., & Fountas, I. C. (1998). *Word matters: Teaching phonics and spelling in the reading/writing classroom.* Portsmouth, NH: Heinemann.

Pinnell, G. S., & Fountas, I. C. (2001). *Leveled books for readers, grades 3–6.* Portsmouth, NH: Heinemann.

Richardson, E. (2003). *African American literacies.* New York: Routledge.

Richardson, E. S. (1964). *In the early world.* New York: Pantheon Books.

Richardson, V. (1990). Significant and worthwhile change in teaching practice. *Educational Researcher, 19*(7), 10–18.

Rio, P. D., & Alvarez, A. (2002). From activity to directivity: The question of involvement in education. In G. Wells & G. Claxton (Eds.), *Learning for life in the 21st century: Sociocultural perspectives on the future of education* (pp. 59–83). Oxford, UK: Blackwell.

Rogers, R. (2002). Between contexts: A critical analysis of family literacy, discursive practices, and literate subjectivities. *Reading Research Quarterly, 37*(3), 248–277.

Rogers, R. (2003). *A critical discourse analysis of family literacy practices: Power in and out of print.* Hillsdale, NJ: Erlbaum.

Rogers, R. (2004). Storied selves: A critical analysis of adult learners' literate lives. *Reading Research Quarterly, 39*(3), 272–305.

Rogers, R. (in press). Teaching (critical) literacy teachers: Reconstructing pedagogical approaches. *Research in the Teaching of English.*

Rogers, R., Light, R., & Curtis, L. (2004). "Anyone can be an expert in something": Exploring the complexity of discourse conflict and alignment in a 5th-grade classroom. *Journal of Literacy Research, 36*(2), 177–210.

Rogoff, B. (1995). Observing sociocultural activity on three planes: Participatory appropriation, guided participation, apprenticeship. In J. Wertsch, P. d. Rio, & A. Alverez (Eds.), *Sociocultural studies of mind* (pp. 139–164). Cambridge, U.K.: Cambridge University Press.

Routman, R. (2000). *Conversations: Strategies for teaching, learning, and evaluating.* Portsmouth, NH: Heinemann.

Schaffer, H. R. (1996). Joint involvement episodes as context for development. In H. Daniels (Ed.), *An introduction to Vygotsky* (pp. 251–280). London: Routledge.

Schneider, J. J. (2001). No blood, guns or gays allowed!: The silencing of the elementary writer. *Language Arts, 78*(5), 415–425.

Schuyler, P., & Sitterly, D. (1995). Preservice teacher supervision and reflective practice. In S. E. Noffke & R. B. Stevenson (Eds.), *Educational action research: Becoming practically critical* (pp. 43–59). New York: Teachers College Press.

Schwartz, R. (1997). Self-monitoring in beginning reading. *The Reading Teacher, 51*(1), 40–48.

Shockley, B., Michalove, B., & Allen, J. (1995). *Engaging families: Connecting home and school literacy communities.* Portsmouth, NH: Heinemann.

Shulman, L. (1986). Those who understand: Knowledge growth in teaching. *Educational Researcher, 15*(2), 4–14.

Silverman, R., Welty, W., & Lyon, S. (1992). *Case studies for teacher problem solving.* New York: McGraw-Hill.

Simpson, A. (1996). Critical questions: Whose questions? *The Reading Teacher, 50*(2), 118–126.

Sims-Bishop, R. (1983). What has happened to the "all white" world of children's books. *Phi Delta Kappan, 64,* 650–653.

Smith, M. W., & Wilhelm, J. D. (2001). *"Reading don't fix no Chevies": Reading in the lives of young men.* Portsmouth, NH: Heinemann.

Smitherman, G. (2000). *Talkin that talk: Language, culture, and education in African America.* New York: Routledge.

Smolin, L. I. (2003). Becoming literate in the technological age: New responsibilities and tools for teachers. *The Reading Teacher, 55*(6), 570–577.

Smyth, J. (Ed.). (1987). *Educating teachers: Changing the nature of pedagogical knowledge.* New York: Falmer Press.

Smyth, J. (2000). Reclaiming social capital through critical teaching. *The Elementary School Journal, 100*(5), 491–511.

Somers, M. (1994). The narrative constitution of identity. *Theory and Society, 23,* 605–649.

Spear-Swerling, L., & Sternberg, R. J. (1996). *Off track: When poor readers become "learning disabled."* Boulder, CO: Westview Press.

Spielman, J. (2001). The family photograph project: "We will just read what the pictures tell us." *The Reading Teacher, 54*(8), 762–771.

Stevens, L. (2001). *South Park* and society: Instructional and curricular implications of popular culture in the classroom. *Journal of Adolescent and Adult Literacy, 44*(6), 548–555.

Sweeney, M. (1997). "No easy road to freedom": Critical literacy in a 4th grade classroom. *Reading and Writing Quarterly, 13,* 279–290.

Tappan, M. B. (1998). Sociocultural psychology and caring pedagogy: Exploring Vygotsky's "hidden curriculum." *Educational Psychologist, 33*(1), 23–33.

Tharp, R. (1993). Institutional and social context of educational practice and reform. In E. A. Forman, N. Minick, & C. A. Stone (Eds.), *Contexts for learning: Sociocultural dynamics in children's development* (pp. 269–282). New York: Oxford University Press.

Tharp, R. G., & Gallimore, R. (1988). *Rousing minds to life: Teaching, learning, and schooling in social context.* New York: Cambridge University Press.

Tomasello, M. (1999). *The cultural origins of human cognition.* Cambridge, MA: Harvard University Press.

Tripp, D. (1998). Critical incidents in action inquiry. In G. Shacklock & J. Smyth (Eds.), *Being reflective in critical educational and social research* (pp. 36–49). Bristol, PA: Falmer Press.

Vellutino, F. R., & Scanlon, D. (1998, April). *Research in the study of reading disability: What have we learned in the past four decades?* Paper presented at the annual conference of the American Educational Research Association, San Diego, CA.

Vellutino, F. R., & Scanlon, D. M. (2002). The interactive strategies approach to reading intervention. *Contemporary Educational Psychology, 27*(4), 573–635.

Vellutino, F. R., Scanlon, D. M., & Sipay, E. (1997). Toward distinguishing between cognitive and experiential deficits as primary sources of difficulty in learning to read: The importance of early intervention in diagnosing specific reading disability. In B. Blachman (Ed.), *Foundations of reading acquisition and dyslexia: Implications for early intervention* (pp. 347–380). Mahwah, NJ: Erlbaum.

Vygotsky, L. S. (1978). *Mind in society: The development of higher psychological processes.* Cambridge, MA: Harvard University Press.

Vygotsky, L. S. (1986). *Thought and language.* Cambridge, MA: MIT Press.

Wade, S. E. (Ed.). (2000). *Preparing teachers for inclusive education: Case pedagogies and curricula for teacher educators.* Mahwah, NJ: Erlbaum.

Wasserman, S. (1993). *Getting down to cases: Learning to teach with case studies.* New York: Teachers College Press.

Wells, G. (2001). The case for dialogic inquiry. In G. Wells (Ed.), *Action, talk and text: Learning and teaching through inquiry* (pp. 171–194). New York: Teachers College Press.

Wells, G., & Chang-Wells, G. L. (1992). *Constructing knowledge together: Classrooms as centers of inquiry and literacy.* Portsmouth, NH: Heinemann.

Wilhelm, J. (1997). *"You gotta be the book."* New York: Teachers College Press.

Wilhelm, J. (2001). *Strategic reading.* Portsmouth, NH: Heinemann.

Wolf, S., Ballentine, D., & Hill, L. (2000). "Only connect!": Cross-cultural connections in the reading lives of preservice teachers and children. *Journal of Literacy Research, 32,* 533–569.

Wood, D. (1998). *How children think and learn* (2nd ed.). Oxford, England: Blackwell.

Wood, D., & Wood, H. (1996). Vygotsky, tutoring and learning. *Oxford Review of Education, 22*(1), 5–17.

Zeichner, K. M., & Gore, J. M. (1995). Using action research as a vehicle for student teacher reflection: A social reconstructionist approach. In S. E. Noffke & R. B. Stevenson (Eds.), *Educational action research: Becoming practically critical* (pp. 13–30). New York: Teachers College Press.

Children's Literature Cited in the Text

Adedjouma, D. (1996). *The palm of my heart: Poetry by African-American children* (Illus. G. Christie). New York: Lee & Low.

Angelou, M. (Ed.). (1993). *Soul looks back in wonder* (Illus. T. Feelings). New York: Penguin Books for Young Readers.

Avi. (1997). *Poppy.* New York: HarperTrophy Publishers.

Bacon, R. (1997). *Our baby* (Illus. D. Fletcher). Crystal Lake, IL: Rigby.

Banyai, I. (1998). *Re-Zoom.* New York: Penguin Putnam Books for Young Readers.

Bloor, E. (2001). *Tangerine.* New York: Scholastic.

Bridges, R. (1999). *Through my eyes* (Illus. M. Lundell). New York: Scholastic.

Bunting, E. (1999). *Smoky night* (Illus. D. Diaz). New York: Harcourt.

Caines, J. F. (1982). *Just us women* (Illus. P. Cummings). New York: Harper-Collins.

Card, O. S. (1977). *Ender's game.* New York: Tom Doherty Associates.

Cartwright, P. (1988). *The wedding* (Illus. I. Lowe). Crystal Lake, IL: Rigby.

Coifer, E. (2001). *Artemis Fowl.* New York: Hyperion Books for Children.

Dadey, D., Jones, M. T. (1996). *Triplet trouble and the field day disaster* (Illus. J. Speirs). New York, NY: Scholastic.

Dadey, D., & Jones, M. T. (1997). *Triplet trouble and the class trip.* New York: Scholastic.

Evans, D. (1997). *Weird pet poems* (Illus. J. Rogers). New York: Simon and Schuster.

Feelings, T. (1993). *Soul looks back in wonder.* New York: Penguin Books for Young Readers.

Flake, S. (2001). *Money hungry.* New York: Hyperion Books for Children.

Gay, M. L. (1999). *Stella, star of the sea.* Toronto, Ontario: Groundwood Books.

Gay, M. L. (2000). *Stella, queen of the snow.* Toronto, Ontario: Groundwood Books.

Gay, M. L. (2002). *Stella, fairy of the forest.* Toronto, Ontario: Groundwood Books.

Greenfield, L. (1978). *Honey, I love and other poems* (Illus. J. Spivey Gilchrist). New York: HarperTrophy.

Grimes, N. (1994). *Meet Danitra Brown* (Illus. F. Cooper). New York: Penguin Putnam Books for Young Readers.

Grimes, N. (1999). *My man blue* (Illus. J. Lagarrigue). New York: Penguin Putnam Books for Young Readers.

Haddix, M. P. (1998). *Among the hidden.* New York: Simon and Schuster.

Herron, C. (1997). *Nappy hair* (Illus. J. Cepeda). New York: Knopf Books for Young Readers.

Hesse, K. (1992). *Letters from Rifka.* New York: Scholastic.

Hesse, K. (1997). *Out of the dust.* New York: Scholastic.

Hesse, K. (1999). *Come on, rain!* (Illus. J. J. Muth). New York: Scholastic.

Hoffman, M. (1991). *Amazing Grace* (Illus. C. Binch). New York: Dial Books for Young Readers.

King, V. (1983). *Grandma's memories* (Illus. G. Rogers). Crystal Lake, IL: Rigby.

Kushkin, K. (1999). *Soap soup and other verses.* New York: HarperCollins.

Lisle, J. T. (2000). *The art of keeping cool.* New York: Aladdin Paperbacks.

McCauley, D. (1990). *Black and white.* New York: Houghton Mifflin.

Marshall, J. (1972). *George and Martha.* New York: Houghton Mifflin.

Mathis, S. B. (1975). *The hundred penny box* (Illus. L. Dillon & D. Dillon). New York: Penguin Books.

Mayer, M. (1983). *Just Grandma and me.* New York: Golden Press.

Myers, W.D. (1997). *Harlem* (Illus. C. Myers). New York: Scholastic.

Park, B. (1997). *Skinny bones.* New York: Random House.

Parker, A., & Parker, C. (nd). *Antarctic seals.* Crystal Lake, IL: Rigby.

Park, L. S. (2001). *A single shard.* New York: Dell Yearling.

Paterson, K. (1978). *The great Gilly Hopkins.* New York: HarperCollins.

Philbrick, R. (2000). *The last book in the universe.* New York: Scholastic.

Prelutsky, J. (1984). *New kid on the block.* New York: Greenwillow Books.

Raschka, C., & Janeczko, P. (2001). *A poke in the I.* Cambridge, MA: Candlewick Press.

Ringold, F. (1991). *Tar beach.* New York: Crown Publishers.

Rowling, J. K. (1998). *Harry Potter and the sorcerer's stone.* New York: Scholastic.

Sachar, L. (1993). *Marvin Redpost: Is he a girl?* New York: Random House.

Sharmat, M. W. (1977). *Nate the great* (Illus. M. Simont). New York: Random House.

Sharmat, M.W. (1989). *Nate the great and the boring beach bag* (Illus. M. Simont). New York: Random House.

Silverstein, S. (1981). *A light in the attic.* New York: HarperCollins.

Simon, S. (1993). *Weather.* New York: HarperCollins.

Spinelli, J. (1993). *Maniac Magee.* Thorndike, ME: Thorndike Press.

Taylor, C. (1992). *The house that crack built* (Illus. J. Thompson). San Francisco: Chronicle Books.

Trueman, T. (2000). *Stuck in neutral.* New York: HarperCollins.

Weisner, D. (2001). *The three little pigs.* New York: Houghton Mifflin.

White, E. B. (1952). *Charlotte's web.* New York: HarperCollins.

Whitehouse, J. P. (1977). *I have a sister, my sister is deaf* (Illus. D. Ray). Bethany, MO: Fitzgerald Books.

Williams, V. B. (1983). *A chair for my mother.* New York: HarperTrophy.

Yolen, J. (1987). *Owl moon* (Illus. J. Schoenherr). New York: Simon and Schuster.

About the Authors and Contributors

Karen M. Amundsen is currently a reading specialist at Shaker Road Elementary in the South Colonie Central School District in Colonie, New York, where she works primarily with third- and fourth-grade students. She remains focused on supporting struggling readers to think critically while reading so that they become more independent learners. She resides in Albany, NY, with her husband and son.

Cheri Collisson started her career in New York 20 years ago teaching kindergarten, then second, and finally fourth grade in the East Greenbush Central School District. She returned to the University at Albany to become certified as a reading teacher. Cheri is currently a reading specialist at the Red Mill Elementary school in East Greenbush working primarily with third-, fourth-, and fifth-grade students.

Cheryl Dozier is an assistant professor at the University at Albany—State University of New York. Cheryl received the 1996 Reading Educator of the Year award from the New York State Reading Association for her work with preservice and inservice teachers. In May 2002, she received a University at Albany School of Education Outstanding Dissertation award. She has a forthcoming article in *Journal of Literacy Research*. Her research and teaching examine the relationships among responsive teaching and readers and their families toward a more just society. All of the research projects examine the multiple layers of teaching, learning, and context.

Susan Garnett is a doctoral student at the University at Albany. She has worked as a reading specialist in local school districts. Her research interest is in teacher preparation. She lives in the Adirondacks with her family. In her spare time she heads for the Maine shores.

Jennifer Grand Steil is a middle-school teacher in the Bethlehem School District in New York State and an adjunct professor at the College of Saint Rose. Her research interest focuses on parent teacher connections at the middle-school level. She recently gave birth to a baby girl, Hannah.

Peter Johnston is a professor at the University at Albany—State University of New York. His research concentrates on the consequences of teaching and assessment practices for the literacies children acquire. He has published over 60 articles, and has authored *Choice Words: How Our Language Affects Children's Learning* (2004) and *Reading to Learn: Lessons From Exemplary Fourth-Grade Classrooms* (2002, with Richard Allington). He is on the editorial boards of *Reading Research Quarterly, Journal of Literacy Research, Elementary School Journal,* and *Literacy Teaching and Learning.* The International Reading Association awarded him the Albert J. Harris Award for his contribution to the understanding of reading disability.

Vanessa la Raé is a doctoral candidate at the University at Albany—State University of New York. Her research interests include the study of literacy events in elementary school as a key site for the production and reproduction of children's sexual and gender relations.

Kimberly Prettyman graduated from the University at Albany with a master's degree in literacy. She currently works at Craig Elementary School as a reading specialist in Niskayuna, New York. She has taught first and fifth grade and serves as vice president of the local area reading council. Kim enjoys canoeing and rock and mountain climbing with her husband, Steve, and spending time with their baby daughter, Zoë.

Rebecca Rogers is an assistant professor in the Department of Education at Washington University in St. Louis. Her research and teaching focus on the development of critical literacy across the lifespan. The National Reading Conference recognized her achievements with the Early Career Award in 2004, and recognized her book, *A Critical Discourse Analysis of Family Literacy Practices* (2003) with the Edward Fry Book Award for "outstanding contribution to literacy research." Rebecca has published articles in *Reading Research Quarterly, Journal of Adolescent and Adult Literacy, Language Arts, Anthropology and Education Quarterly,* and the *Journal of Literacy Research.* She is on the editorial review boards of numerous research journals. Rebecca worked as a reading specialist in an elementary school and in an adult education classroom. She also served as the program coordinator for a volunteer adult literacy organization in New York.

Lisa Strolin-Smith is a reading specialist in the Brewster Central School District in Brewster, New York. She is currently pursuing her doctorate at the University at Albany. Over the past three summers she has enjoyed teaching at the University Literacy Lab where she continues her interest in studying the construction of new literacy learning for both teachers and their students and how it shapes the classroom environment.

Index